I have often said that Kim Bearden is the smartest and fiercest person I have ever known. You will agree after reading *Fight Song*. Kim's wisdom and grace will help you find passion and purpose, and her capacity for love will capture your heart. You need this book. We all do.

      Ron Clark, award-winning educator, bestselling author,
           cofounder of the Ron Clark Academy

Fight Song is a powerfully penned work of art, revealing what makes one a warrior in this thing called life. Kim Bearden's vulnerability, poured out throughout this book, encourages the reader to look within and draw their own strength from their current circumstances. Bearden's gift of helping one muster up courage and embrace their purpose is second to none. In all honesty, if the words on these pages don't renew your passion, uplift your spirits, and inspire you to stand up and press forward — fight — you might want to check your pulse. *Fight Song* is for YOU!

    Tara Martin, educator, director of PR and communications, keynote speaker, author

Kim Bearden's latest book is a true testament in rediscovering the strength we have within ourselves to overcome and endure. Countless readers will find solace in this book and deem it as the battle cry they need to persevere.

    Dr. Valerie Camille Jones, Presidential Award for Excellence in Math and Science winner

Throughout my educational career, Kim Bearden has remained a constant source of hope, wisdom, and love for me. As an educator, I've observed that people unconsciously forget that teachers have personal lives as well. Maintaining the balance of being a great educator while maintaining the other facets of our life can be stressful. In *Fight Song*, Bearden eloquently shares how all of us can take our own adverse situations and become stronger individuals for the world!

      Michael Bonner, award-winning educator, speaker, author

Unflinchingly raw yet intimately joyful, *Fight Song* is Kim Bearden's narrative through heartache, healing, and unceasing love. Galvanized by unwavering fortitude and resolve to rise, Bearden invites readers to experience how truth and peace can illuminate our darkest moments. Bearden's warrior spirit radiates from each page, capturing the infinite and transformative impact of selfless surrender, strength in unity, and service to others. Prevail and punctuate *your* personal journey as you ignite passion, uncover power, focus on peace, and exude purpose. Triumphantly liberate *your* battle cry and live empowered. Your *Fight Song* awaits you.

    Stephanie Frosch, pre-K/early childhood special education consultant

Fight Song is a treasure that reminds us: obstacles do not block the path because they ARE the path. Kim Bearden's remarkable journey reminds us to honor and celebrate both who were are and how we got there. She has turned trials into tribulations, and her story — sent straight from the heart — just might inspire you to discover, sing, and share your own battle cry with the world.

Wade Whitehead, educator, speaker, and National Teachers Hall of Fame inductee

Kim Bearden's latest book is a gift that speaks to the soul of anyone who has ever traveled a difficult journey, personally or professionally. Kim is a woman of grit and grace whose authenticity and courage enfold you the moment you open the book. Within the pages of this deeply personal narrative, you will discover a wise and compassionate friend who will challenge you, inspire you, laugh with you, and cry with you . . . and when you go to sing your own fight song, you will realize that Kim Bearden has always been in your corner cheering you on!

Brian Sinchak, president, Lakewood Catholic Academy

Kim Bearden pours her heart onto these pages to help us grow. With each page, you can feel it in your spirit! Kim connects us with practical tools and mindsets to help navigate life, encouraging and empowering us all to be the best version of ourselves — to be our own version of extraordinary.

Dr. James Whitfield, principal, Heritage Middle School

Kim has a light that shines from within and bounces right off the pages of this book. *Fight Song* shares her journey to a place filled with peace, love, and joy while encouraging us to recognize and appreciate our own.

Dr. Natalie Odom Pough, college professor of mathematics education

Kim Bearden's newest book, *Fight Song*, fills us with hope, resilience, and a workable plan to achieve a life of impact. She shows us how using a positive mindset to confront the negatives in life can change our song to one of affirmation and joy. A definite must-read!

Dr. Penny Ferguson, National Teachers Hall of Fame inductee
and educator for fifty-one years

Kim speaks directly to the reader's soul in her new book, *Fight Song*. She challenges you, as the reader, to reflect upon the difficult experiences in your life, and to use them to identify your personal truths, modify your mindset, and discover the inner strength you may not have seen in yourself. Kim's personal stories will touch your heart, and her powerful words will lead you to identify, proclaim, and amplify your true purpose . . . one that will make a positive difference in the lives of others.

Holly Ehle, kindergarten teacher/literacy specialist

FIGHT SONG

Six Steps to Passion, Power, Peace, and Purpose

KIM BEARDEN

FIGHT SONG

Six Steps to Passion, Power, Peace, and Purpose

Fight Song: Six Steps to Passion, Power, Peace, and Purpose

© 2020 Kim Bearden

This book is available at special discounts when purchased in quantity for educational purposes or as premiums, promotions, or fundraisers. For inquiries and details, contact the publisher at books@daveburgessconsulting.com.

Published by Dave Burgess Consulting, Inc.
San Diego, CA
DaveBurgessConsulting.com
Library of Congress Control Number: 2020935724
Paperback ISBN: 978-1-951600-18-1
Ebook ISBN: 978-1-951600-19-8
Cover design by Chad Beckerman

Cover photo by J. Amezqua
Interior design by Kevin Callahan/BNGOBooks.com
Editing and production by Reading List Editorial: readinglisteditorial.com

To my precious family —
Scotty, Madison, Phakamani, Sabelo, and Sisipho.
You are my love, my life, my greatest joy.

And to Mona —
You exemplify the woman I strive to become.

*There is a song within you
just waiting to be sung.*

Contents

Author's Note

Soon after submitting the final manuscript for this book, the entire earth changed, due to the COVID-19 coronavirus. As I write this, schools have been canceled indefinitely, and cities are placing residents on mandatory quarantines; thousands have become sick. Unprecedented fear and anxiety have taken hold across the globe, and I do not know what our new normal will be. However, it is my fervent prayer that the words in this book will still provide readers with healing, hope, and strength in the days ahead. I pray that we will all find our warrior within and continue to fight together for the future of our families, communities, nation, and world.

Foreword

Before you read this journey of survival, inner strength, and victory over defeat, I'd like to give you a glimpse of this story through my eyes as Kim's daughter. I am a firsthand witness to the strength of a woman who fought fear and found faith, a woman who turned darkness into light, despite all odds against her.

As far back as I can remember, my mother, Mim, immersed me in the blissful world she created for me. Without keeping me sheltered from the pain of this world, she made it so I always knew that I could handle anything with her by my side. I knew that God would never give me more than I could bear and that my life was made for a divine purpose and for a reason that could defy all triumphs or tragedies. I was sure we were destined for greatness and that happiness would prevail, despite the pain and obstacles we faced. Life has a funny and tragic way of showing you what needs to be seen. Through the sadness and darkness, life's lessons are revealed, and you learn that deep-rooted wisdom and beauty were made for you all along.

Perhaps it is hard to understand, but I am grateful to have endured the pain — the storm — that eventually cleared to reveal the most beautiful rainbow. The feelings of fear and confusion that were sometimes our life forced me to fight the odds and see all that was within me. A child is taught much by witnessing her mother overcome — through seeing her faith and moral compass put into action. To truly feel the unfolding of trauma and the process of healing as she experienced it did more for my overall understanding of life and love than any verbal explanation, sheltered reality, or naive fairy tale ever could have.

Before Mim wrote this book, she asked me if it was okay to reveal some of our story. I told her it is her duty to do so. My mother has a gift for igniting a fire in the lives of others, and I know that as you read her words, you will gain the strength that she has always instilled in me. I found the capacity of my soul through my mother's. She imprinted my self-value upon my heart. The warrior in her has become the warrior in me. And she will help you find the warrior within yourself.

She is your best friend.

She is your survivor.

She is your fighter.

She is the voice telling you your worth.

She is the one who is wild and fearless and strong.

She is the one who laughs at those who doubt her.

She is the one who lets vulnerability in to teach
    her a lesson,
        only to become stronger in the end.

She is the one who yells louder when voices silence her
    and who listens quietly when wisdom speaks.

She is the one who uplifts the ones who are
    hurting the most,
        even if they are angry in their discourse.

She cannot be broken, for she has risen from the ashes.

She summoned strength when the world had its
    back turned.

She found the deepest inhale and exhale after
    gasping for air.

She moved mountains with her arms tied behind her back.

She found grace and loved herself after her heart had been
    cold and hardened.

She is a lion, brave and strong.

She is my mother.

Madison Stewart Hunt
Warrior. Fighter.
Daughter of Kim Bearden

Prologue

2001 I am lying on my side in that foggy state somewhere between asleep and awake. A heavy weight presses on my chest as if someone is pushing a cinderblock upon it. I want to roll to my other side, but I cannot — the weight becomes heavier and sharp, and I become paralyzed by fear. I realize that I have stopped breathing. I am falling, drowning, suffocating. I force myself to take in air slowly, rhythmically, while pressing my palm to my chest. The anxiety is overwhelming me, but somehow I am still able to convince myself that it will pass. It always does. I will be okay . . . it will be okay . . . we will be okay. I call out to God to heal me, protect me, hold me. The warmth of my tears soothes me. I cradle my pillow tighter and beg my body to return to sleep. It comes slowly, fitfully, until the light of dawn filters through my blinds and I am forced to get up and face the day that lies ahead.

I had a secret.

My marriage was in shambles, and I had discovered that my then-husband had betrayed me in numerous ways with numerous women. I was devastated and broken into a hollow shell of my former self. My world as I knew it had gradually fallen apart until I didn't know how to climb out of my tunnel of despair. Each day, I swallowed the pain while attempting to navigate the torrent of emotions that surged through me. Pain and anger seeped into my soul and eventually magnified into humiliation and fear of discovery. But we can all only hide behind an illusion for so long — the mirages eventually disappear, and the truth comes to light. Compounding my misery, I had allowed my fear of others' perceptions to define me as I relentlessly strived to

> *Eventually, I learned that each time I was knocked down, my brokenness empowered me to grow stronger than before.*

fulfill a stereotype of how I thought the perfect wife, mother, and teacher should look and act. But perfection is unattainable, and my inability to deliver left me feeling small, insignificant, powerless, and utterly alone.

Many nights, I would find myself curled on the floor of my closet, my body racked by sobs that I muffled with my hand so my little girl wouldn't hear my sorrow. Over and over again, the same song played on my mind's soundtrack until I finally grew sick and tired of being sick and tired. From deep within me, an inner fight and mindset flickered to life, sparking a flame that steadily grew into a new anthem, a new kind of strength. I knew I had to fight my way back; I had to choose living over existing.

My situation is not unique — all of our lives are a mixture of harmony and discord. At some point, we all feel broken, defeated, or exhausted; we resent being overworked, overwhelmed, undervalued, or underappreciated. People endure marital strife, betrayal, financial struggles, professional challenges, addiction, health issues, oppression, abuse, loneliness, and concerns for our children or other loved ones; unfathomable heartbreak plagues our world. Things happen to us that are completely beyond our control. But we must never forget that there is no shame in pain and struggle, for it is universal.

Eventually, I learned that each time I was knocked down, my brokenness empowered me to grow stronger than before. Eighteen years have passed since that chapter of my life unfurled, and I now realize that, if I hadn't endured so much strife, I might not thrive as much as I do now. In the depths of my darkness, I became enlightened. In the pages that follow, I want to show you how to do the same. I will share the thoughts and actions that changed my life and helped me find passion, power, peace, and purpose.

Your story is different from mine, but it is my prayer that my words will empower you, uplift you, and perhaps help heal your hurt. This is not a teaching book—it is a heart book. However, when our hearts are healed, we are empowered to do the most extraordinary things for children, for family, for loved ones, for everyone we encounter. In order to shine brightly, we must first see the light. If you are already shining brightly, my hope is that my words will encourage you to cast your radiant warmth upon all you encounter. Don't worry—this is not *Chicken Soup for the Depressed Soul*. Rather, this is my fight song. And it can be yours, too. Cue the music. There is a song within you that is waiting to be sung.

chapter 1

Identify

Modify

Amplify

Unify

Fortify

Battle Cry

First, we must IDENTIFY our worth, our gifts, and our truth. In doing so, we are better able to navigate life's obstacles.

It was November 2007, and the doors of Ron Clark Academy had been open for just two months. Our mission had been ambitious from the start: to deliver the highest-quality educational experience through advanced rigor, engaging teaching methods, and a passionate climate and culture, all while teaching visiting educators how to do the same in their own classrooms. This November day was one of the very first professional development sessions for teachers, and they had spent their time observing our lessons and attending our workshops.

At the conclusion of the day, the sound of djembe drums reverberated off the old brick walls as the students' cheers set the space ablaze with joy. "Slide certify, certify!" they chanted, as one by one dozens of visiting educators shot down the two-story electric-blue slide, the centerpiece of our school. The slide is a symbol — a reminder to have no fear, to be bold, and to embrace taking a different path in life. Upon exiting the massive tube, each received a *Slide Certified* sticker to commemorate the event and our time together.

As educators assembled throughout the lobby to watch the others complete their descent, many were overcome with giggles; others had tears pooling in their eyes. Tears are not uncommon on training days — visiting our school is often described as an emotional experience, and many are moved by our students and the love that abounds throughout our building. However, there was one young teacher standing apart from the others, desperately trying to wipe away the huge droplets that sprung from her eyes.

As I approached her, I held out my arms, and she readily collapsed into them. "Sweetie, are you okay? Talk to me," I said.

"Everything was just so wonderful," she sobbed.

Wow, this day really went well, I thought . . . until she finished her sentence.

"And now I feel so much worse than when I got here this morning!"

To be honest, that was the last thing I expected her to say. I was devastated to hear this, so I responded, "Oh, no! Then we failed you. Our goal is to uplift you, support you, and provide you with tools to help you serve your students better. I am so very sorry."

"It is not your fault," she said. "You see, Kim, I am going through some terrible things in my own life." She went on to tell me about her family struggles, her financial struggles, and her relationship struggles, before adding, "Many days I feel like I'm a terrible teacher, and now after being here, I know one hundred more things that I could or should be doing, and the reality is that I don't have it in me to do a single one of them. I know you probably think I am horrible for saying that. I love my students so much, and I just wish I could be more like these other teachers. It makes me feel so guilty. Everyone here seems to have it so much more together than I do."

Even if you are not a teacher, I am sure that on some level you can relate to how this sweet teacher felt; we have all felt weight beyond our ability to carry it. She was completely undone, and she was doing her darndest to keep pushing through. She was struggling trying to balance personal trauma with her professional life. As she talked about what a terrible teacher she must be, her sobs grew louder — so much so that I had to gently take her elbow and lead her into an empty classroom to talk.

When she spoke of her pain, I realized that many of her circumstances were beyond her control. It was not her fault she was experiencing the current trials in her life. However, she blamed herself for her inability to do all she wanted to do as a teacher. She was comparing herself to every other educator, and she had convinced herself that everyone was better than she was. She spoke of guilt as if it were a heavy cloak she could not remove. However, the fact that she spoke of her love for her students and her desire to be so much for them told me what I needed to know. She needed to grant herself some grace. So much of teaching is heart, and hers was obviously bursting with love for her kids, even if she was hurting and exhausted.

I started to ask her questions about her kids, her school, and her favorite lessons. Her eyes lit up as she shared stories about them. I took her hand, stopped her midsentence, and said, "I would have loved for my children to have had a teacher like you. You love your students, and your strength through your trying circumstances is an inspiration." This time she wept in gratitude. The cloak had lightened ever so slightly as I validated her, enabling her to find some peace in the shadow of her pain. I hoped that my words helped her realize her value, despite the challenges that had been placed in her path.

We are all like that sweet teacher at times. When life knocks us down, we must stop to identify our worth, our gifts, and our truth. In doing so, we are better able to navigate life's obstacles.

Worth

Just because something bad happens *to* you, it does not mean that something is wrong *with* you. My personal faith is very important to me; however, I have never subscribed to the belief that God will bless me with fame, fortune, and a life free from pain if I just believe more, try harder, and pray more. Look at the mother who is watching her child battle cancer; the man who is discriminated against because of the color of his skin; the child whose parent has been tragically killed; the woman who was abused; the teenager who is bullied because of his sexual identity; the grandmother living in abject poverty; the family fleeing their war-torn country. There are many books that will promise you a perfect life if you just have more faith. This is not one of them. I find that to be dangerous thinking. It implies that if you are struggling, it is your fault. Some struggles might be the result of our choices and behaviors, but quite often they are not. Some of the most beautiful, amazing, faithful people I have known have endured the most pain. I fervently believe in prayer, and I live by faith. But faith does not eliminate life's battles; rather, it sustains and soothes, enabling us to emerge stronger than before.

When you catch yourself thinking that there must be something wrong with you, you must stop and identify what is really true about you. In my former marriage, I was often called names; I was made to believe that I was less than. At first, I tried to protect my heart, put on a brave face, and push down the hurt, but when you hear the same melody playing again and again, it becomes a part of you. Did he cheat on me because there really was something wrong with me? The words I heard were etched into my consciousness. As I lay on that closet floor one night, I cried out to God. *Enough, Lord. I have had enough!* I prayed. And then the answer I needed filled me — not audibly, but deep within my soul: *Kim, **you** are enough. You are uniquely created with gifts and talents that can profoundly affect the lives of others. It is time to get to work.*

So, get to work I did.

If we allow another's words to become our internal dialogue, we spiral down into a place where we risk turning our false fears into reality. If you keep telling yourself you can't, well, you probably won't. If you keep telling yourself you don't deserve it, you will probably never get it. If you keep telling people that you aren't good enough, they will start to believe you.

Do you have your own self-defeating mantra?

- If only . . .
- If I had . . .
- I failed because I am . . .
- I am worthless because . . .
- I can't because . . .
- If they only knew . . .
- I won't ever achieve that because . . .
- I don't deserve it because . . .
- They are better than I am because . . .

> You have purpose that exceeds your understanding — you must only be willing to receive this truth.

Look, we all have flaws and issues, and we all fall short at times. But when you feel small, you must stop and take inventory of who you really are. Deep inside of you, there is a voice that whispers that you are good enough, strong enough, smart enough . . . you are enough. It is that part of you that wants to overcome, wants to succeed, wants to fight, and wants to heal. Do you hear it? Or do you drown it out with your hypercriticism of yourself? You have purpose that exceeds your understanding—you must only be willing to receive this truth.

Too often, we are our own harshest critic, yet we freely offer abundant mercy to others. Think about someone on this planet whom you admire greatly—a noble, honorable person whom you and others respect beyond measure, someone who truly makes the world a better place. Do you have someone in mind?

Do you admire this person because of these traits?

- Wears size 4
- Has amazing hair
- Achieved perfect SAT scores
- Has multiple degrees from impressive universities
- Has lots of money
- Sings well
- Has washboard abs
- Wears designer clothes
- Keeps house immaculate
- Has an impressive job title
- Drives a luxury car
- Dances professionally
- Has a huge social media following
- Raised perfect, attractive, over-achieving children
- Has an adoring spouse

Or do you admire this person because of these traits instead?

- Love
- Peace
- Patience
- Kindness
- Goodness
- Gentleness
- Self-control
- Determination
- Compassion
- Understanding
- Wisdom
- Insight
- Charisma
- Generosity
- Courage
- Joy
- Strength
- Dedication
- Helpfulness
- Positivity
- Loyalty
- Honesty
- Humor

Now, surely some of you might be thinking, *Well, Kim, I thought of Beyoncé, and yes, she is rich, sings well, has several mansions and cars, has phenomenal abs, and has epic clothes. And I admire that.* And you would be right—she is awesome, and I'd love to have lunch with Queen Bey, borrow her clothes, and have those abs, too. But I would also argue that much of Beyoncé's success grew from the second list. And maybe she was given such success because she has a unique purpose meant just for her. Perhaps instead you thought of a CEO who has had incredible business achievements. This, too, is admirable, but I would again suggest that some of the qualities from the second list probably led to the characteristics on the first one.

My point is this: we can't all be Beyoncé or the CEO of a Fortune 500 company, but we can all be our own version of extraordinary. You might not be able to carry a tune, but you can be loving, kind, helpful, good, and hardworking. Yet we often diminish ourselves by thinking that the first list is what gives us value. Yes, there is only one Beyoncé, but there is also only one you.

You must take time to be still and reflect upon all of the honorable traits that you do possess—traits you might have dismissed as being unimportant, yet ones that you assign value when others demonstrate them. Are you a good friend? Do you uplift others? Are you supportive? Hardworking? Positive? Loyal? Do you seek to understand? Do you make people laugh? If so, you are the kind of person whom I would love to have lunch with and befriend, even if you haven't seen your abs since scrunchies and parachute pants were in vogue.

Change your mantra.

- I am worthy because . . .
- I deserve to be treated better because . . .
- I am able because . . .
- I am a good person because . . .
- I can accomplish many things because . . .
- I can make the world better because . . .

Confidence

It was our first year in operation, and the news crew assembled in the lobby, anxious to start filming a story about the innovative strategies at the Ron Clark Academy. I smiled and watched as one by one the producer, reporter, and cameraman told Ron how much they admired him, his story, his work in Harlem, and the movie about his life. He graciously thanked them all and replied, "Well, let me tell you why RCA is here in Atlanta. It is because I wanted to create this school with the smartest woman I know. This is Kim Bearden, the cofounder and executive director of the school."

It was then that I realized I had been standing outside of their circle. I stepped forward, stood upright, and shook each hand. Up to that point, I remember thinking, "This is so great that they are here to learn about the school. Ron is so amazing." At no point did I consider that I had a role in the narrative; I had diminished my own worth, even though Ron kept attempting to redirect the spotlight onto me. I would do this time and time again during that first year, much to his chagrin. When I think back, my actions projected weakness and insecurity. I diminished myself—no one else did it to me.

To be clear, our school is about kids, not Ron or me. If you had watched me that first year, you would have seen me pouring everything I had into my work and into our students and staff to build a school like no other. However, you might also have seen me hold back time and time again, only to have Ron grab my arm and pull me back to his side. Ron Clark is truly one of the most amazing humans I have ever known, and I admire him with all that I am. However, there was a reason he asked me to join him in starting the school — he saw that he needed my talents and my gifts working together with his to make our school a reality. I knew that I was a strong teacher, but he saw something in me that I hadn't yet acknowledged within myself. Now I see it so very clearly, and I step forward, head held high, and project the confidence of someone who helped build a magical place from nothing more than a dream. I own that, embrace that, and give thanks to God for the opportunity.

Are you standing in the shadows of your own success? Are you hiding your light from the world? Too often we do this, and in dimming our light, we plunge ourselves into darkness. Please don't be an "I'm just" kind of person.

- I'm just a teacher.
- I'm just helping.
- I'm just a stay-at-home mom.
- I'm just the assistant here.
- I'm just here in case they need me.

Be an "I am" kind of person instead.

- I am proud to be a successful teacher.
- I am here to help.
- I am able to take care of that situation.
- I take care of others and empower them to be their best.
- I am able to make this happen.
- I am here to make sure things go smoothly.

Confidently identifying your gifts and talents is not arrogance; it is appreciation for your worth. But be very clear: once you have identified them, you are required to use them. It is your purpose. Change the station from the static that keeps you from acknowledging your value, and celebrate what is good and true about you.

1997 I sit cross-legged on Madison's bed brushing her golden hair until it shines. X is downstairs drinking himself into oblivion again, and I need to keep her with me upstairs, away from him. He blasts Pearl Jam and sings so loudly that it penetrates the door, but both Madison and I pretend not to hear it. Does she notice? Does she know what I am trying to do? I read to her, lie with her on the bed, tickle her back, whisper to her, and pray over her until she falls fast asleep. I need to keep her in her bedroom so she won't see him stumbling about the house. I don't want either of us to interact with him because, inevitably, even the sound of my voice will set him off, and his shouting and name-calling will begin. It is always about placation . . . don't do anything to upset him, anger him, or incite his rage. Keep everything calm, Kim. But underneath our family's veneer, an explosive storm always simmers, and it is matched by the desperation that swirls within me.

I convince myself that Madison and I can create our own separate reality, one where I fill her nights with fairies, Barbies, crayons, and stories; one where we watch Disney movies to drown out the sounds of his incoherent ramblings. She is my entire world, and I want to protect her, to shield her from the darkness that permeates our truth. His binges are often days, even weeks at a time, and I find myself praying that he might have another business trip so we can once again convince ourselves we lead a carefree existence in a house filled with joy.

Sometimes he begs for forgiveness, saying he will do better, be better. Sometimes he blames his drinking on everyone in his life, including us. Sometimes he is kind, loving, and charming; sometimes I am afraid for us to be in the room with him. Sometimes he will go weeks without drinking at all, and I cling to a glimmer of hope that things will be okay and he really might change, but the weeks that he is free of alcohol are the weeks that he is really using illicit drugs without my knowledge. The illusion of calm is overshadowed by an evil that I cannot yet fathom or comprehend, for addicts are sometimes masterful actors and liars. He never hits either of us, but the words he uses are still painful blows that I feel with every part of my physical being.

Why do I stay? How can I — a strong, smart woman — allow this to be my reality? I often ask myself that same question, but the honest answer is that I do not know.

I think I will feel guilty if I leave, but I feel even guiltier for staying. I hope he will change, even though I know he will not. I believe that my daughter needs a father, even though he is a horrid example of what one should be. I think that others will judge me, even though I know I have done nothing wrong. I think that I can somehow love him again, even though all I feel is hatred. I think I need to honor the commitment of marriage, even though he has violated every part of our covenant. At times, I even think that perhaps I am the crazy one, though deep inside, I know that it is he who has lost touch with reality.

Peace

Perhaps the story above makes no sense to those who have never experienced living with an addict or in an abusive situation. It makes no sense to me as I write it, but I share it so that some of you will know that you are not alone, and there is hope; you can escape.

I needed to identify the mistruths I had convinced myself to believe and identify my reality. I had to seek what was true, real, honest, and good. I needed to trust and hope for my future and release the worry that held me captive in order to find my strength. I had to fight.

Truth: This was not what was best for my child. It was not best for me. He would not change. I deserved better. I was capable. This was not my fault. I was a good mother. I would triumph over this and lead a life of joy again. I would find peace.

Worry is a thief — it steals our joy and fulfillment. I should know, for I am the proud descendant of a long line of worriers. My grandfather, Pa, was a classic worrier in every sense. He was a tender, gentle man who truly hated the dark and who lived with the fear that something would happen to his family. Every summer we would go to Virginia Beach to see him, and even if it was August, Pa would wear long sleeves, pants, and a fedora because he feared the

Madison and me

sun. (Actually, he was much smarter than most of us on this one.) When he grew older, his anxieties worsened — when there was a solar eclipse, I remember him holding his hand over his eyes all day long because he heard it was dangerous to look at the sun. I loved my Pa so very much, and so did my mother — his daughter.

If worrying were an Olympic sport, my mother would have won many medals and acquired several endorsement deals. Only her worrying didn't start in her old age; it was a constant throughout my life. When I was a little girl and I needed to cough or sneeze, I would run into the bathroom and run the water so my mother wouldn't hear me, diagnose me with pneumonia, and keep me home from school.

Among the things my mother worried about are the following:

- Icicles: One landed on Aunt Beulah's head and rendered her deaf in one ear.
- Wet feet: I had to wear Wonder Bread bags on my feet under my snow boots so I wouldn't have to sit in school with wet feet and get sick.

- ATMs: "They knock people in the head at those machines. You are not getting an ATM card and getting killed."
- Bicycles: If I rode even three yards past our cul-de-sac, I would be hit by a semitruck.
- Raw cookie dough: "You will get salmonella."
- The internet: This is a tool used by deviants and perverts to look at porn.
- Drowning: I was forced to use the Bubble—a large, Styrofoam, egg-shaped floatation device worn on your back—until a completely inappropriate and humiliating age.
- Driving: My mother's car had less than a thousand miles on it. She used it to go to the grocery store and back. This became an issue when they closed the nearest grocery store, and she was no longer able to make the trip using only right-hand turns.

My mother also worried about rats (I inherited this one from her), horseback riding, and anything that could inflict bodily harm. Perhaps this is why I grew up to have a thrill-seeking nature and love to skydive, parasail, horseback ride, and hang glide.

My mother's biggest passion—that is, concern—was the weather. At any moment, she could relay the temperature, the forecast, and the barometric pressure like a professional meteorologist. This obsession would override every other topic of conversation, even ones of great importance to me. Here are snippets from actual conversations we had:

"Mama, guess what? I am going to have the opportunity to take my students to the Oprah Winfrey Leadership Academy for Girls in South Africa! We are going to be there for two days, and I will have the honor of teaching there and conducting professional development!"

"That is so wonderful, honey. You always make me so very proud, but isn't it unbearably hot in South Africa?"

Or another of my favorites:

"Mama, I am actually going to be given the Disney Award at the Shrine Auditorium in Los Angeles. There will be celebrities there, and the whole thing will be televised. It is going to be amazing, and you and Daddy get to come!"

"I am so proud of you — I cannot wait to call my friends. Will it be safe for us to go? Isn't Los Angeles where they have all those earthquakes and forest fires?"

Or, another instance:

"Mama, I had the most wonderful trip to New York. I'm so excited — I have my first book deal. I am going to be published!"

"You know I'm always proud of you, but how did you stand the cold while you were there? The Weather Channel said it was freezing. Were you careful? You know that they hit people in the head there."

My mama was also kind, loving, and devoted to her children, and she was an incredible mother and grandmother who loved unconditionally and gave without question. I must also share that she taught me to be one who loves deeply and laughs often. I lost my precious mama to Alzheimer's, and every single day my heart aches to be with her again. My mama is now dancing with angels, and I think that she, too, would tell you that she wasted time worrying about things that never came to pass. I hope she is looking down on me and laughing with me at some of her more absurd moments. However, I also wish that she hadn't spent so much of her life worrying.

Worry kept me from moving forward with my life for too long. I worried about raising my daughter, Madison, alone. I worried about my bills. I worried about how I would possibly be able to do things on my own. I worried about what others would think. I finally learned that my worry didn't change or fix anything; it just stole my joy.

I had to learn how to stop myself from plunging into a downward spiral of negative what-ifs:

- What if I fail?
- What if I am alone?
- What if I am not good enough?
- What if people talk badly about me?
- What if I let everyone down?
- What if I lose everything?

Now to be clear, when my life fell apart, I had real drama and reasons for concern. I had to devise a plan for how to put my life back together.

However, I changed my negative what-ifs to positive ones, and it made a huge difference.

- What if I succeed? Wouldn't that be amazing?
- What if I embrace being able to take care of myself instead of relying on someone else?
- What if I discover that I am stronger and more capable than I ever knew?
- What if I stop concerning myself with what others think of me?
- What if I lose everything? Is it things that really matter?
- What if I focus on making myself proud instead of making others proud of me?
- What if all of my fears come true and I still prove triumphant?

Even if the worst possible scenario happens, you can still emerge victorious. You might be stronger, better, and even happier than before. Sometimes, there are scenarios that exceed the normal realm of pain that you cannot change and that you did not cause. There are so many things I will never understand, and those who overcome such sorrow and struggle amaze and inspire me. But sometimes, we allow even small setbacks to cause us to spiral downward into hopelessness.

If you find yourself panicking, worrying, or hurting, ask yourself if the situation will matter a week from now . . . a month from now . . . or even a year from now. Oftentimes, our momentary pain is just that . . . momentary. Worry keeps you from seeing the truth clearly. It distorts our ability to seek solutions, to believe in ourselves, to hope for the future. It is a deceiver who steals peace, replacing it with anxiety that weakens the soul.

Truth

Sometimes this anxiety truly is based upon difficult, painful truths — truths that we must find the strength to correct, change, confront, or even leave behind us. Realize that facing the truth is the first step to finding a solution. The solution may be hard — it may seem impossible — but you must not avoid it; you must wrestle with it, deal with it, or even fight it so you can live your best life. For me, the truth really did lead to my being set free.

Facing the truth is the first step to finding a solution

2000 After putting Madison to sleep, I go outside and walk toward the driveway to retrieve my book bag from my car. The stars above shine brilliantly, and the crisp autumn air makes me shiver. It's a beautiful evening, and my heart feels light. It has been one of the good days. As the coldness of the driveway penetrates my socks, I wonder why I did not choose to put on shoes before going outside.

I meander past X's car en route to mine when a small light catches the corner of my eye. It seems to be coming from the behind the driver's seat, so I open the door to find its source. Upon further inspection, I see that it is coming from inside the back-seat pocket, and I reach in to find a small Nokia cell phone. Cell phones are relatively new technology, and I'm confused to discover this one — it does not belong to me or to X . . . or so I think.

I push the button, and the screen lights up again . . . from a text message.

I begin to scroll. My body is still, but inside I am falling, falling, falling . . . into depths where I cannot breathe. I am drowning. At some point, I collapse onto the frigid concrete, where I sit for minutes that grow into what might be hours. I wrap my arms around my knees and hug myself as I rock back and forth, back and forth.

I have told myself that the alcoholism is a sickness and that the verbal abuse springs from its grip upon him. But here in my hand, I hold evidence I do not want to see. Text after text with woman after woman on a phone that is obviously used to perpetuate a double life. Even at his worst moments, I didn't know he was capable of such deceit, such debauchery, such betrayal. I suddenly throw the phone into the grass — as if it is a fire that has burned my hand. I swallow my sobs and pray, and then I grow still.

A new awareness rises within me: the phone is a gift. I will choose to be grateful for it. I walk into the damp grass and retrieve it, wiping the moisture from every key. I jump into my car and grab a notebook so I can *transcribe every text message into it (this is before phones were enabled to take screenshots). Then, I simply sit in the back seat as calm washes over me. I wipe my tear-stained face and stride into the house where X sits on the couch watching television. I silently walk over to him, place the phone in his lap, and walk up the stairs. I do not scream; I do not shout. He does not come after me. Deep inside, I have already begun to plan: I will eventually force him to leave, but I will be certain to gather every bit of necessary evidence. I will be methodical. I will gather financial records; I will search computers. A chorus of resolutions fills my consciousness. There will be sleepless nights and lapses of calm in the months ahead; worry will sometimes paralyze me with its grip. This, however, is the beginning of the end. I make myself a promise: one day, I will have a completely new life. And once free, I will never turn back.*

As I sat in that cold driveway that night, "Why me?" looped as an endless refrain in my mind. It was not fair — not fair at all. This was just too much. But then "Why me?" turned into "Why not me?" What makes me so special that nothing bad can happen to me? Bad things happen to good people all the time. I realized that it was just my turn, and how I chose to deal with it would be what would define me. That was when the pain transformed into a plan. When we ask, "Why me?" we allow ourselves to be a victim. I was done being a victim; I would be a victor. This was my life, and I would no longer pretend it was something it was not.

Grace

Confession: I am tired — not only at this moment, but quite often. I am a wife, mother, administrator, teacher, and, like many educators, I have a few side gigs, too. How could I not be tired? And you don't have to be married with kids to have a lot on your plate. We all do. Oh, I am fulfilled and happy, but I have been known to fall asleep in public places — jaw dropped, drool spilling out of my mouth — if I have just a moment to sit still. I cannot physically juggle everything that I need to do and want to do, and I think it is okay to admit that. Moreover, I think it is important to admit that. We are often told that if you just try harder, you can "have it all!" Maybe you can, but certainly not all at once. There was a wildly popular commercial for Enjoli perfume that played way back in 1979, and the jingle was so catchy that I still remember it to this day. I know that some of you were not even born in 1979, but the message is one that the media still conveys to us.

In the commercial, a beautiful woman in a business suit sings about bringing home the "bacon" as she waves cash at the camera. Next, we see her in her robe, joyfully cooking dinner for her family. Finally, she claims she will never let her husband forget he's a man as she sways in a beautiful negligee, all while looking sexy, sultry, and overjoyed. It all looks like a fabulous life, but I wonder . . . Who was bathing the kids and putting them to bed while she was never, never letting him forget he was a man? Who cleaned up the kitchen? Bacon leaves a lot of grease. Oh, and after eating all that bacon, you surely need to hit the gym. She had a lot of outfit changes for the day—when is she getting that laundry done? Does she take it all to the dry cleaners? Does she ever forget to pick it up? Does she have to catch up on paperwork before collapsing into bed? Is there a school function that night, or do her kids have practices to go to? Do her children need help with homework? Does her husband need to talk about his day, too, and feel like she is listening? Did she remember to check on her elderly parents to make sure they have groceries? Does she ever worry about how to pay the bills? Does her floor sweep itself? Did anyone walk the dog? If Enjoli perfume takes care of all of that, then I am buying!

Yes, I bring home the bacon, and sometimes I cook it. More often, my husband cooks it, or we order out. I hope I always make him feel like a man. But laundry is spilling onto the floor of my closet, my emails are breeding, and I have been looking for one of my favorite boots for a good three weeks now. My car hasn't been washed in three months, and my trunk is so full that it looks like I am opening a thrift store out of it. I have been carrying papers that need grading around in my book bag for three days in hopes that they will magically grade themselves. My go-to home outfit is baggy sweatpants and an oversized T-shirt. I am still devastated that I missed my son Phakamani's soccer game last week where he kicked the winning goal because I was out of town giving a speech. I missed my son Sisipho's play, too, when giving another speech. On Saturdays, I take care of my dad who has Parkinson's; he lives an hour away, and it is heart-wrenching to see him diminishing. Since I am gone all Saturday, I feel guilty for not being with the rest of my family. When I am with the rest of my family, I feel like I should be with my dad. When I am at home, I feel like I need to be catching up on work. When I am at work, I feel like I need to be doing more at home. I am grateful for my life, and it is filled with joy. But in order to get to that place, I had to let go of guilt and realize that, sometimes, something has to give, and that is okay. Look, if someone visits my house and takes issue with the dishes in my sink, who really has the problem?

Despite all of this, I recognize my privilege. But I don't have it all. You can't have it all, either, and just maybe you shouldn't. Why? Because once you have it all, it is no longer enough, and you want more. Plus, if you ever do have it all, shouldn't you be giving some of it away? How do you even define *all*? Does it mean that you have the perfect job, spouse, home, body, prestige, and income? Do you need more stuff? What would make it so perfect? I hope this doesn't make you feel depressed — I hope it makes you feel empowered . . . and relieved. The idea of *all* is an ever-changing illusion that we create . . . and it diminishes the gratitude for what we really do have. Instead of obsessing about what is missing, focus on what is present; instead of focusing on what you haven't accomplished, celebrate what you have managed to do.

Yes, you absolutely can have a life filled with love, laughter, purpose, passion, significance, and success. But you can and will drop the ball sometimes, and that is okay. To be clear, I am a highly driven person. I am fierce. I am even proud to have many refer to me as a badass. I want to do more, be more, and grow more. However, I have learned to give myself a break and to focus on what I think is the most important to me — my family, my students, my loved ones, and my work with education. And I still fall short at times. I still battle mom guilt — the struggle is real. There are times when I simply cannot be in two places at once, and I have to do my best. Therefore, I have learned the importance of being present — fully present — in whatever role I am operating.

For example, if you are a teacher, when you are in that classroom, your focus has to be those kids. See them, believe in them, teach them, love them. You don't have to stay on campus until ten at night to be a good teacher; it is better to give 100 percent of yourself while you are there and then go home to

> *The closest we can get to ALL is to be ALL IN in the moment — to be fully immersed in our relationships, our passions, our purpose.*

your family than to stay at school all night and miss being there for your own kids. Don't let another teacher's pictures of her classroom on social media make you feel like your students are not receiving as much from you if you are pouring 100 percent of yourself into them while there. It is more about what they see in your eyes than what others see on your social media feed. When you are home, it is more meaningful to spend a few extra minutes sitting at the table talking than it is to do the dishes at that very moment. Or do the dishes together. What if you don't even have time to sit at the table together because your schedules are so different? Then find time in the car, before bedtime, any time. Books and media sometimes portray women who juggle everything with ease, but they gloss over the fact that those women sometimes have a whole team of nannies and assistants, something that most of us do not have the luxury of having.

The closest we can get to *all* is to be *all in* in the moment—to be fully immersed in our relationships, our passions, our purpose. The rest is icing. Icing is great, but you can't have too much of it without the cake.

If you are tired, please rest. Find time for soul care. Be still . . . sit and stare at a wall if you need to. Journal, walk, hide in your closet if it is the only quiet place in your house. When we don't stop to be still, the results permeate our thoughts, actions, mood, and patience. We tend to see more of the negative than the positive. We focus on what we don't have instead of what we do. We often want more instead of realizing that our lives are full of blessings, even in the most difficult of moments.

As I write this, it is November. I just took a moment to scroll through social media and look at the fabulousness of others. Some takeaways:

- I, too, can lose thirty-five pounds in two months if I would just cut back on carbs.

- My husband really should leave me romantic notes so I can post them.
- My kids are great, but they weren't elected to student council. And they haven't been accepted to Ivy League schools, either.
- My classroom decor has not changed for fall, and everyone else's has.
- My gosh — there are some amazing teachers out there. I should do more.
- I really need more throw pillows.
- I really need to get some cuter outfits for winter.
- I should be at the beach.
- I should be ashamed that I never really learned how to cook well.
- Why can't my plants grow like that?
- Why does her glass of wine look so much better than mine does right now?

Do you see my point? I have allowed myself to feel this way before. Have you? It is a dangerous mental trap; we "compare and despair" instead of granting ourselves grace. Too often, we assume that others' lives are perfect and only ours is lacking. We must remember that social media is a highlight reel — it is the highs, not the lows; it is usually the joy, not the sorrow, that is posted. It is not just the pictures that are filtered — lives are, too. There is a whole life being lived between the posts, complete with laughter, struggle, happiness, and heartache.

No one's life is without some type of pain. Yet, we often look at others' lives as superior; sometimes, we even let the ugliness of jealousy start to take root in our lives. Jealousy is one of the most all-consuming and destructive of all emotions, and in a sense, jealousy is selfish and self-centered. If you are constantly jealous, you are saying that *you* deserve something more, *you* want it for *you*, *you* wish *you* had it to make *you* happier, and *you* wish the other person didn't have more of it than *you*. It's all about *you*.

The jealous-minded person's self-talk goes something like this:

- I should have their financial status.
- I should have kids like hers.
- I should look like she does.
- I should have had his job instead of mine.

- I deserve that recognition more than she does.
- I should have a husband like hers.

But honestly, should you really? Look, I have just spent an enormous amount of time telling you to step into your spotlight and that you are uniquely and wonderfully made. This is true. But does that mean that you deserve a life other than the one you have been gifted with? Here's the clincher: if you had someone else's life, you might wish you had your own back. The life you envy might have more pain, suffering, heartache, and heartbreak than you can imagine; the reality you desire might only be an illusion. Focus on what you do have, not what you do not.

Realize that there is a difference between wants and needs. I always want the newest style of Converse high tops, but I don't need them. Do you need the newest phone or want it? Do you need a new car or want it? A bigger house? A grander vacation? It is okay to want and even to get, as long as we keep our desires in check and realize the difference. Sometimes losing everything we want can even help us understand what is truly the most important of all. When we identify life's truths, it is then that we are really ready to live.

Notes

♪ Realize that just because something happens to you, it does not mean something is wrong with you

♪ Identify your value, your gifts, and contributions.

♪ Offer yourself grace and embrace the qualities you have that you admire in others.

♪ Change your mantra from self-defeating to self-appreciating language.

♪ Claim your worth.

♪ Change from being an *I'm just* to an *I am* person.

♪ Recognize your truth, and release worry.

♪ Avoid the negative *What-ifs*.

♪ Identify unhealthy comparisons and focus upon what you do have.

Change Your Tune

♪ Be still and reflect upon all that is good and noble and true within you. Write these traits down and refer to this list often. Replace your "I'm just . . ." statements with "I am . . ." statements.

♪ Make a list of worries that you carry with you and replace them with truths.

♪ Make a list of unhealthy comparisons that have made you feel less than and acknowledge the blessings you have been given.

♪ Identify ways that you can replace wanting it *all* with being *all in* during the moment.

Identify

(Modify)

Amplify

Unify

Fortify

Battle Cry

chapter 2

When we MODIFY our thoughts and actions,
we are better equipped to handle
challenging situations.

———

2002 Over a year has passed since the unveiling of the deceit. As I
sit on the beach with my twelve-year-old daughter,
Madison, I hold her warm hand inside of mine. Our family is supposed to
be on vacation together — I have not yet broken free — but another fight
erupted, and Madison's father disappeared hours ago.

The setting sun paints the horizon with pink and purple ribbons while
the ocean breeze dries the tears spilling down my cheeks. I study her hand
like I always do, memorizing every contour and line. Her fingernails
always remind me of perfect little seashells, so smooth and white. I stroke
Madison's sun-kissed hair as I rest my head on her shoulder. My heart
is bursting both with love for my little girl and with the pain of betrayal,

uncertainty, and fear. I try to swallow it, only to feel the sting in my chest. I want to protect her from every dark thing, to shield her from knowing all that has happened.

Finally, she whispers, "Mim, you have to leave him. You are so smart and kind and loving and good, and you deserve so much more. I know you are staying for me, and I cannot be happy if you are just doing this for my sake. You have done everything you can. It is time."

I put my head down, unable to speak. I remind myself to keep breathing as I watch my tears drop onto the sand. There it is . . . my precious daughter knows, despite my best efforts to hide it all. I believe in the sanctity of marriage, and I believe in trying everything possible to make it work. And I know that I have. Her words validate me — I feel that God has just smiled down upon me and granted me the grace to know it is okay. I am okay. We will be okay because I am capable, kind, smart, loving, and good. There will be much work ahead, but I am resolved and ready to fight my way back to myself.

We walk down the beach and back to our hotel, hand in hand. In the middle of the night, her father comes back. Madison and I snuggle tighter in the bed together and feign sleep. The next morning, we arise before he does, pack our things, and head to our new version of home — a place where I will no longer allow him to stay, a place where we will compose a new life.

I had finally identified and embraced my truth, my value, and my worth. In doing so, I was empowered to change my circumstances. Modifying my thoughts and my responses to pain enabled me to fight for the passion, power, peace, and purpose in my life. We all have the capacity to do this, with setbacks both big and small.

Mindset

Thirty-two fifth graders proceeded in a single-file line through Washington Dulles International Airport, like baby ducklings headed to water. Their faces shone with anticipation. This was their class's first overnight trip, and they had been studying every possible fact about our nation's capital in preparation for this momentous occasion. The forecast had predicted snow, making their excitement palpable. A class trip + monuments + a hotel stay + snow = BLISS.

Jordan Still bounced down the terminal in her SpongeBob SquarePants hat, capturing the attention of a local television reporter. We gathered around Jordan as she explained on live television why we were in DC. The reporter then asked our students if they were ready for a blizzard. "Yes!" they all cheered, and I grew somewhat nervous. Blizzard? For real?

Real it was. Within hours, what is now known as the Snowpocalypse of 2009 dropped 16.4 inches of snow on Washington, DC, bringing the city to a complete standstill. It shut down the city's restaurants, museums, and monuments. We were staying at a Holiday Inn Express, a hotel that provided a light breakfast but had no restaurant. We had no food and no transportation, and we were completely snowbound.

The hotel management gave our group a meeting room so we could all hunker down together, and after every last dry biscuit and muffin on site had been consumed, we knew it would be a long weekend. We went into solution mode. Mr. Kassa, Mr. Bruner, and Mr. Adams put on layers upon layers of clothing and left in search of food, while Ron, the kids, and I played every game that could possibly be played when you have no game boards or game pieces. We acted, we danced, we laughed, we told stories. We held an impromptu talent show; we competed over random trivia. After an hour trek through the snow, our courageous staff returned with a meal fit for kings: Cup-a-Soup, Spam, Cheetos, cinnamon buns, beef jerky, and the last remaining paninis from a local gas station food mart. It was all they could find, and we devoured it with giggles and appreciation. We bundled up and went outside and held an epic snowball fight, and when we returned to the warmth of the room, we huddled closely together with even more stories to tell.

What could have been a disastrous school trip turned out to be one of the most memorable experiences of the students' time at our school—they still talk of it ten years later. What made it so memorable? We identified the reality of our situation and modified our mindset. When we modify our thoughts and actions, we are better equipped to handle challenging situations.

Instead of coining the experience a disaster, our incredible staff promoted it as an epic adventure, one that we were in together. We would defeat nature, hunger, and boredom. We would be victorious! And we were.

Do you allow your present circumstances to dictate your contentment with life? I know I have done so. If my circumstances were good, I was happy; when something went wrong, I was sad. The issue with this is that every single day circumstances beyond our control can make a day go terribly downhill. It is not just the major life challenges that can do this — sometimes it is the day-to-day inconveniences that disrupt and steal our contentment. If you can't fix your circumstances, try to fix your thinking. Let me show you how it works with two versions of two different scenarios:

Negative mindset

Geez. This traffic absolutely sucks. What is wrong with these people! Oh, you aren't going to let me over? Really? Is your day really going to be ruined if you take ten seconds to let one car in front of you? Jerk. I am going to be late. I need to get there. Will you people please GO?! The traffic isn't moving up ahead, either! ARGH! This is why I hate driving in Atlanta.

Modified mindset

Oh, wow. The traffic is horrible. It looks like there is an accident ahead, and I might be late, but I sure am thankful that I am not in that accident. I hope no one was hurt. I am grateful I have a car to drive. I am fortunate that I am driving that car to a job. Stressing is not going to make me get there any faster, so I just need to breathe. Let me find a good song on the radio since I will be sitting here a while!

Negative mindset

I hate, I mean I *hate* grading these papers! Did these kids even study? Did they even listen to what I said? I am done with them all. I should just give them all workbook pages for the rest of the year because they obviously don't care at all. That is what is wrong with kids today — they just don't care like they used to. And that is what is wrong with education and this job and my life.

Modified mindset

I sure don't enjoy grading these papers, but every job has negatives, right? I am so disappointed in some of these grades — I am frustrated. I guess I need to really look at what they missed and see if I can find a pattern. I think it would help if I talked to some of the students one-on-one to ask why they missed some of these questions. A year from now, I won't remember these grades, but I will remember these students and how much I care about them. I need to find a way to adjust my plan to get them on track!

Thinking this way does not mean that you swallow your emotions — that is not healthy. Do I ever scream, punch a pillow, or cry in frustration? Yes, I absolutely go there. The key is that I don't allow myself to stay there. Look, I told you that I spent many nights on my closet floor, and at the time I wasn't thinking, *Gee, I am so grateful for carpet.* I allowed myself to express my rage and pain, and you should, too, if necessary. But doing so day after day after day takes you down a dark tunnel where it is harder to find the light. If traffic is bad, slap that steering wheel and sigh, but then adjust to the modified mindset after you have let off a little steam.

Trust

Sometimes we have been so conditioned to think a certain way that we cannot see the forest for the trees; we hang onto negativity, fear, worry, doom, and gloom. We tell ourselves that we are less than, we are unlovable, we are going to be hurt, we are going to fail. But we must allow ourselves to see things through a positive lens—a lens of hope. If we do not, we can miss receiving some of life's greatest blessings; we can push people away who are meant to be a part of our lives. I was still struggling to figure this out when I hired Scotty Bearden.

> We must allow ourselves to see things through a positive lens — a lens of hope. If we do not, we can miss receiving some of life's greatest blessings

I walked out of my office at my previous school to interview an applicant for the after-school soccer coach position and found him standing there. His smile was disarming, and when he shook my hand, I felt electricity surge through me. My neck and face grew hot, despite the fact that I was thirty-nine years old. I was completely undone. Scotty Bearden had come highly recommended as a coach, but I was not expecting this feeling, this reaction to him. *I am the principal, for heaven's sake! Get it together, Kim!* I thought.

I did hire Scotty Bearden to coach our students, and I was, indeed, smitten. However, I remained professional, as did he. Three months after he was hired, our school's Latin teacher was ready to go on maternity leave, and despite my best efforts, I couldn't find a suitable substitute anywhere. (Good Latin teachers don't exactly grow on trees.) I shared this in a conversation with Scotty, and he replied, "I can do it. I took Latin for four years." Having recently sold a restaurant he co-owned, Scotty had the time to take the position.

So, for several weeks, Scotty worked down the hall from my office. Whenever he came to ask me questions, I would blush like a silly middle-school girl. One afternoon, he offered to set me up with one of his friends so I could get back into the "dating groove." I was devastated. *I guess he isn't too interested in me!* I thought. *I am too old. I have too much baggage. He is out of my league.*

I later learned that Scotty was actually very interested, but he felt that I would never be interested in him. Plus, there was that whole employer-employee issue for the few weeks that he would be the substitute teacher. We did, however, do some things as friends, such as play pool and go to dinner, spending hours and hours laughing, talking to each other, and getting to know one another. It wasn't until he'd finished his temporary position as the Latin teacher that he actually asked me on a date, and when he finally kissed me, well — I felt it in my toes.

Perhaps the most interesting part of the story is one that I didn't even share with Scotty for many years. I had kept it as my own little secret; it seemed entirely unbelievable. A few months before I met Scotty, I was home alone, contemplating my future and feeling quite lonely. My divorce had not yet been finalized (once I found X after he disappeared, he initially refused to sign the papers), but I had been on my own for a while. Online dating was gaining popularity and had just become a widely acceptable way to meet people. Out of curiosity, I went to an online dating site to see if there would even be any options for me out there. I thought that I was most definitely going to be alone for a long time — I was approaching forty years old, and I had a heck of a lot of emotional baggage. I had no intention of joining the site, but I was still able to see the men's bios and photos because the site allowed you to "browse" for free as a means of luring people to subscribe. I guess it was the dating version of window shopping.

I typed in *Atlanta*, and countless bios appeared. Before I knew it, I had spent a large part of a lonely Saturday evening looking and reading. The whole process left me even more depressed than I had been when I began. Finally, I clicked on a picture of a ruggedly handsome man — there was a photo of him standing atop a mountain, but it was hard to make out his face. There was also a photo of him sitting on the couch with an older man, presumably his father. I read the bio, and as I did, I was struck by the man's apparent honesty. He talked about his strengths and his weaknesses with great candor; others had portrayed themselves as far too wonderful to be real. I remember thinking, *Well, maybe one day I will meet someone like him — someone honest and trustworthy.* As I shut off my computer, I thought, *Two hours of searching, and only one appealed to me. Those aren't good odds. I will probably be alone forever.*

A few months later, when Scotty and I were nurturing our friendship, he came to my office after school. As I mentioned, he had offered to set me up with one of his friends. I told him that I'd consider it. He then asked me how else I planned to meet people and suggested that I join an online dating service. I told him that I didn't think I could post my photo on a site like that. What if one of my students' parents saw it?

Scotty said, "Have you ever even looked at one of those sites? They are really well done — lots of people use them now. They aren't what you think."

"Really? Um . . . no, I haven't ever looked at one." Okay, so I lied.

"Here, let me show you," Scotty said, and he opened up his laptop. He pulled up the same site I had explored that night months before and said, "I've used this site before. Here, I will show you my bio."

And there it was: the handsome, rugged man atop a mountain and the man on the couch with his father. It was the bio I had been attracted to months before . . . it was Scotty. I tried not to gasp. I tried to act natural. But it was at that precise moment that I knew I would marry Scotty Bearden. I knew it with absolute certainty, even though he had not even asked me on a date.

Over the next few months, my instincts proved to be correct. I was broken, and he was patient. I had built up walls, and he gently waited for me to take them down. I didn't trust, so he went out of his way to reassure me. I questioned everything, and he provided answers. I was skeptical, and he understood. I shared dreams, and he supported them. He was beautiful, kind, gentle, and calm. He loved kids, animals, and helping others. My daughter, Madison, adored him, and he healed her heart as well. He was my calm in my unpredictable world; he set my troubled soul at rest. He seemed too good to be true, but he was real. I was terrified, but I surrendered my heart and chose to believe in him, in us, in hope. At age forty, I married him in a beautiful ceremony, surrounded by family, friends, and students.

I had to learn to think differently about who I was and what I deserved. I knew that I didn't need a man to complete me — I could take care of myself. When I was finally able to recognize that truth, I was ready to receive the blessing of this relationship. I did deserve a man like him. All these years

The best day

later, I try not to let a day go by when I don't tell him and show him that I love, respect, appreciate, and cherish him.

Perspective

In addition to my roles at RCA, I travel across the country as a professional speaker. In doing so, I have experienced many adventures, but one that happened several years ago stands out for being what could have been called a terrible, horrible, no-good, very bad day.

My itinerary called for me to take a flight at half past six in the morning, land at half past eight, rent a car, drive for two hours, and meet the district's administrators for lunch at noon before speaking to a few hundred teachers. A typical engagement, or so it would seem. I arrived at the Atlanta airport in plenty of time, although it was definitely too early to feel human.

When I prepared to go through security, however, I discovered that I didn't have my driver's license. Big mistake.

I remained calm and went into my get-it-done management mode. I pulled out everything I had with my name on it: my SkyMiles card, my debit card, a business card. That's it — I had nothing else. I travel light. So, I pulled up the RCA website page with my photo and bio and prayed for mercy. I approached the security agent and pleaded my case. I told him that I had teachers counting on me and that I had to get on my plane. Thankfully, he did have mercy on me and escorted me through the security checkpoint. Crisis averted — or so I thought.

As soon as the plane took off, I realized the second obstacle: How would I rent a car without a license? Throughout the flight I thought about it, but I figured I could get the car the way I'd gotten on the plane, and I refused to panic. Well, let's just say that the car rental place wasn't as sympathetic. In fact, I went to four different counters, only to be told "no" over and over. I knew I was losing time, so I approached a limo service counter and just accepted the fact that things were about to get expensive. However, they were out of cars. At this point, I wasn't the least bit surprised.

By this time, I knew it was too late to call the school district because, even if they left to come and get me right then, I still wouldn't make it there on time. With no idea what to do, I shared my sorrows with the limo service representative, who offered me a solution: "I have a buddy who drives his own cab. Want me to call him?"

And that is how I ended up with the opportunity to bond with Leroy on a two-hour, $203 ride. Leroy really was the sweetest little old man — he had nine great-grandchildren, and I could tell that they all must love him dearly. Leroy was eighty years old and still driving, and he had the cutest way of giggling when he said something he found humorous. As we drove, the weather became worse and worse — thunder and lightning and a continuous downpour that made driving a challenge — but I felt safe and comfortable, and I even dozed off for a while.

We arrived at the high school at eleven thirty. My day was now back on track. I took Leroy's number — he would have to take me back to the airport, too — and then entered the high school and told the receptionist I was there for an event at noon. She was lovely, and she offered for me to go relax and dry off in the conference room. (I had gotten completely soaked on the way to the front door.) I chilled out, answered some emails, and gave thanks for the fact that my day had now turned around.

At 11:55, I walked into the lobby to wait for my escort, but he was nowhere to be found. I called the cell number I'd been given and left two messages. The bell rang, and students flooded the halls from every angle; it was apparently an early release day so the teachers could attend my training. Students were everywhere, so I decided to go out the front door to see if my escort was waiting there. The rain had slowed to a drizzle, and hundreds of kids were scattering for buses and carpool lines.

And then I had to break up a fight. Two boys started shoving each other and talking about their mommas when I shouted, "Stop that right now!" in my best teacher voice.

They hadn't noticed me before, and when they turned to me one asked, "Do you work here?"

I yelled, "Does it matter?" It was an effective enough diversion, and by this time, the campus security had shown up.

Finally, my phone rang. When I answered, my escort said, "Where ARE you?"

I explained where I was, only to be told, "We changed the event to the elementary school. Didn't someone tell you? Please just drive on over here now."

I had to confess that I could not drive over for lack of a car. Fortunately, one of the coaches came to my rescue and took me there. By the time I arrived, I'd missed the luncheon. I was mortified. But I kept telling myself, "Do not allow all these things to make you have a bad day. You have to be positive to be helpful to these teachers."

I gave my speech, and the group was great. Things were on the upswing. Afterward, I called Leroy and informed him of my new locale. Another two hours and $203 dollars later, my bank account was depleted, and I was back at the airport. Leroy had once again safely driven me through treacherous weather, and I knew I'd be home in a few hours. I still had no driver's license, but this was a tiny airport. Surely, getting on the plane would be a breeze.

Well, it was as if TSA had been waiting all year for such a cataclysmic event. Once again, I approached the agent with my items: my SkyMiles card, my debit card, and my business card. This guy wasn't amused. When I showed him the website, he responded, "Ma'am, we cannot accept websites; you could have made that website just to falsify your identity." Gulp.

"Please step aside and follow me." I was escorted into a roped-off area where I was asked to complete a form with numerous questions about my name, date of birth, address, and more. I waited and waited for someone to arrive, but it was obvious that I would be there a while. Finally, the supervisor approached me. This gentleman was intense to say the least, and I began to think I'd be missing that plane home. "Ma'am," he said, "I'm going to have to call headquarters and ask you a series of questions to confirm your identity." The supervisor called someone on his cell and proceeded to spew a series of numbers — if I didn't know better, I'd say he was fantasizing that he alone was giving the codes to the president to launch a nuclear attack.

His questioning began. "Please state your full name and your social security number."

As I answered, he repeated my answers to the Powerful Oz on the other end. Upon hearing the response, his expression became startled. "Ma'am, do you go by any other names?"

Oh, yeah. I forgot that my social security number was still under my previous name. Oops — I had never changed it.

I explained, and he moved on. However, his skepticism was visible.

"Ma'am, please state the address of your residence prior to your current address."

What? At the time, I had lived in the same house for fifteen years, and for the life of me, I couldn't remember that previous address. I stumbled, I joked, and I told him that I thought it might be Winding Lane. He wanted the street number, and it just wouldn't come to me. I was actually getting nervous.

Finally, I said, "Sir, I am sorry, but I can't remember. I've lived at my current address for over fifteen years."

His next question: "What is your husband's date of birth?"

At this point, I was flustered, and I actually gave the wrong year. "April 20, 1964!" *I blurted. Too bad it was 1967. Numbers have never been my forte. I corrected myself when he raised an eyebrow at me, but it was obvious that things were not going well.*

Next question: "Please state the first and last name of one of your neighbors."

Okay, well, this was a real problem. You see . . . I didn't know my neighbors. Before you judge me, please be aware that my house was on a street with several rental houses, and the residents changed often. Also, I worked really long hours. And my good friends who had lived next door had moved away. . . . Crap—that does sound really bad, doesn't it?

"I'm sorry. Um—I don't know," I whispered, my face growing hot.

Supervisor: Pause . . . pause . . . pause . . . "Ma'am, do you expect me to believe that you have lived in the same house for fifteen years and you don't know a single one of your neighbors?"

So, there I was, failing a test on my own life. Finally, I said, "Sir, I appreciate all you do as a TSA supervisor, and I realize that it is your job to keep all of us safe. I understand why you are asking me all of these questions, and I apologize for not being able to answer them all with accuracy. Honestly, I have had a horrible day. I had to pay $406 in cab fare, I've been lost, I've been poured upon, I've broken up a fight, and I don't feel well at all. I am a teacher, and I need to be back in my classroom tomorrow. If it is at all within your power to let me on that plane, I would be eternally grateful." Although reluctant, he eventually let me through. I ran through the terminal and made it onto the plane right as the jetway door was being closed.

Once I finally arrived home and recounted my adventure to my husband, I finished by saying, "Do you know what I take from all of this?"

Scotty answered, "That you should know our neighbors?"

Sigh.

What I did tell him was that I had been exhausted before that trip, and if I had driven four hours in that treacherous weather, there was a good chance I would have had an accident. I believed that I needed that time to sit back, enjoy Leroy's company, and relax. I truly think that sometimes a series of obstacles are put in our way to protect us or set us down another path, and I just wasn't meant to drive that day. It was an expensive lesson but one that I chose to embrace. Perhaps you didn't get that job. Perhaps that partner broke up with you. Perhaps you missed that flight. Maybe you lost that phone number. Maybe you got so lost that you missed that life-changing appointment. And maybe, just maybe, you were supposed to. A detour of even just a few moments has the power to change the course of your day, your week, and possibly even your life.

And, okay — I admit it. I need to meet my neighbors.

Looking back on this story, I now realize that I should be grateful to the TSA agent for taking his job seriously. He is responsible for keeping us all safe. I also acknowledge that perhaps it was my privilege that enabled me to get on that plane in the first place. However, throughout that eventful day, every time something went wrong, I thought, "Of course!" But then I shook it off and went into solution mode. Crying, whining, or getting angry would have gotten me absolutely nowhere. Taking it out on others I encountered would have made them have a bad day — I would have been spreading negativity to a world in desperate need of joy. I chose to believe that my day was meant to unfold just as it had — possibly even for my own good. When you learn to think this way, you will be amazed at how differently you start to see your reality.

Look, sometimes we all have "terrible, horrible, no-good, very bad days." But if you modify your mindset to one of acceptance and trust that maybe there is a good reason for your strife, you will stop sweating the small stuff so much. Little annoyances just don't hold that much weight, and your appreciation will increase dramatically. Lemons become lemonade . . . or better yet, grapes become wine! Modifying your mindset can empower you; it can even give you courage to take a leap of faith.

> Modifying your mindset can empower you; it can even give you courage to take a leap of faith.

Courage

It came as no surprise to anyone who knows me that I wanted to jump out of an airplane at fourteen thousand feet to celebrate my forty-fifth birthday. My husband, Scotty, made the arrangements, and we drove about forty-five minutes outside of Atlanta to a massive, open airplane hangar filled with tons of instructors in their late twenties and early thirties. (Think surfer dudes appareled in awesome skydiving suits.) Guns N' Roses' "Sweet Child O' Mine" reverberated throughout the hangar as the instructors carefully rolled and packed a sea of parachutes. The chutes carpeted the floor, creating an ocean-like rainbow that fluttered with the September breeze.

After signing multiple forms releasing the company from any liability in the event of our untimely deaths, Scotty and I people-watched while we waited our turn. We found ourselves playing Frisbee with a group of dogs, their tales wagging frantically with enthusiasm. Finally, I was called to meet my tandem instructor, Miki. Miki was a former New Yorker who had been jumping for eight years. I instantly liked him. He was funny and charming, yet extremely professional as he went over the procedures with me. I instinctively knew that I'd be safe. Miki explained how we would be jumping in tandem—he would be attached to my back by straps, and he would be in control at any time if I needed him. However, he would also allow me to steer the chute and guide us as we made our descent. We carefully reviewed all of the procedures, strapped on our gear, and headed to the runway.

We climbed onto the small plane—eight jumpers, eight tandem instructors, and some videographers. I was ready and oh so excited! My assigned videographer interviewed me as the plane rose higher and higher. Five thousand feet, seven thousand. . . . There was no door on the plane, so as we rose higher and higher, the cold air enveloped us. Music blared on the plane, too, and as Aerosmith told me to "Walk This Way," I prepared for my jump.

Miki asked me how I'd like to exit the plane. I had two choices: I could either do a front flip or just jump. Without hesitation, I chose the flip. When we reached fourteen thousand feet, I kissed Scotty, and Miki strapped himself to my back. We approached the door, and the powerful wind whipped at my hair and face.

And then I jumped.

Out we went, tumbling into the heavens. We were actually above the clouds. The freezing air whipped through my hair, and I truly felt like I was flying. The plane roared above me, the wind enveloped me, and all I could do was laugh. Not just a little, either. I was tickled beyond belief. We dropped in freefall for a short while through the clouds. The air was so cold, the sky so blue, the clouds so beautiful, the moment so exhilarating—I just couldn't stop laughing. Honestly, I just don't know how anyone could experience something like that and deny God's majesty. It was a deeply profound and spiritual experience for me.

After the freefall, it was time to pull the chute. Upon doing so, we rose slightly higher, and then complete silence filled the air. We were floating, and Miki and I began to talk. He told me how to steer the strings, and he pointed out various things on the ground below. I was in awe. He then asked, "Do you like roller coasters?"

"Yes!"

"Okay, hold on then!" he exclaimed as he pulled the strings in a way that made us go around and around as we descended. As we finally approached our landing, Miki just told me to relax and he'd guide me in. We descended lower and lower, until I finally slid onto the ground as gently as if I were on a slide on a preschool playground.

Afterward, Miki and I gathered in the field with the other jumpers. As I thanked him, I was still laughing. He said, "Kim, I've literally done hundreds of tandem jumps in the past eight years, and you are the very first person that I've ever been able to hear laughing over the roar of the airplane. Thank you — I will never forget it!"

I had to be willing to take the plunge, or I never would have experienced one of the most exhilarating, joyful moments of my life. That jump fueled a fire in me . . . the same fire that fuels my desire to do more, be more, and create more moments for others.

Sometimes, we have to take a leap into the unknown to fully experience the possible joy and fulfillment of purpose that awaits us . . . and it can be far scarier than jumping out of a plane at fourteen thousand feet in the air.

> Sometimes, we have to take a leap into the unknown to fully experience the possible joy and fulfillment of purpose that awaits us.

Ron Clark and I met when we were both Disney Teachers of the Year, and he had so much passion and energy for life that I could not help but be affected. In my previous books, I have shared how we cofounded the Ron Clark Academy, but there is something I haven't mentioned: It was scary. Maybe even terrifying. I walked away from job security and everything I had ever known to build the school with him. For a year, Ron's condo doubled as our office. We would sit at our desks and dream, plan, ponder, and plot. Some thought I was crazy. Some thought we were both crazy and that our school would never succeed because we were a nonprofit and all of our students, even those who had never had academic success, would attend on scholarship. However, we believed in our dream, we believed in our students, we believed in teachers, and we believed in ourselves. It took us years to open our doors, and there were many months after we opened when we worried about making payroll. However, people saw our hearts, and then they, too, believed.

I am not suggesting that you be reckless, quit your job, and pursue a job as a stand-up comedian. Actually, if you are that funny and it is your dream, maybe you should. All comedians started somewhere, right? My point is this: sometimes, we are called to do something big, something bold, and something extraordinary, something that will modify the course of your life in profound ways. However, how do you know whether to step forward or hold back?

I can only tell you what has worked for me. My major life decisions have come down to one word: peace. If I am in turmoil, I seek peace of mind. When I pray and weigh my options, the one that gives me peace is the one I pursue. I can be afraid, overwhelmed, and unsure. I can wonder if I have the time, talent, resources, or knowledge to accomplish it. But when it is the right decision, a peace that surpasses understanding takes hold, no matter how difficult the circumstances. I draw upon that peace for strength; I use it as the foundation for my courage. A year after I married Scotty, I told him I was going to quit my job and work full-time on starting RCA with Ron. We had no savings. I had no money left in my twenty-year retirement fund — I had to use it when I was a struggling single mom. Scotty's response? "Of course."

Peace.

Choices

Many years ago, I mentored a young teacher, and quite frankly, she was a hot mess. She was talented and book smart, but, oh me, she attracted drama, and when it didn't find her, she would go looking for it. She was constantly in spats with her friends because so-and-so told so-and-so what she had said, and she couldn't believe her friends (the ones she also gossiped about) would betray her like that. She dated a few different men with different names, but I swear they were all the same guy — arrogant, disrespectful, and unmotivated. All of this seemed to stem from the fact that she was always caught up in a storm of unhealthy, repetitive behaviors. It took me a full year to gently help her realize that most of her drama and stress was self-inflicted. However, it also stemmed from a childhood that was not her fault in any way. As a result, she

Sometimes we are victims of our circumstances, but other times we create our problems through our own bad choices.

was insecure and didn't understand that she deserved better. She sabotaged herself without even realizing why. I bet you know a person like her. It is even possible that the person is you.

Sometimes we are victims of our circumstances, but other times we create our problems through our own bad choices. When we find the courage to identify this pattern, we have to modify our behavior if we hope to find peace and purpose. You know that thing that you keep doing that causes you drama and stress? Stop doing it. Just stop. Or ask for help from someone who can help you stop. Are your words painful weapons? Do you use them to inflict pain and destroy? Then hush. You know those people that you keep spending so much time with? The ones who make you less than? The ones who encourage you to make poor decisions that diminish your success or your view of yourself? Or the ones who gossip, slander, and entice you to judge or hate? Stop hanging around them. You know that thing you are addicted to? Please seek professional help if you need it — you deserve to get better. It might be hard, it might even seem impossible, but don't stop fighting for your peace. You are worth it. Changing our behavior requires truthful self-reflection — you must acknowledge your strengths but also identify what you need to change. We often tell ourselves lies to justify our illusion of reality:

- It won't really hurt anyone.
- No one will find out.
- It doesn't really mean anything.
- Everyone does it.
- Others get away with it.
- It won't really affect me or anyone else.
- Doing it will make them like me more.

In truth, our poor choices do hurt others in addition to ourselves; we often cause pain for the very people who love and care about us the most. Please don't sell yourself the lie that "they will never find out." They most likely will, and even if they do not, there is a separation—a distance—that seeps into the relationship and manifests itself as a loss of connectivity. Our actions can steal peace, destroy trust, diminish self-worth, fracture faith, and even shatter souls. When we choose to self-destruct, we leave wreckage behind, even if we do not intend to do so.

Reaction

On the night of our very first open house at RCA, my heart was full of joy and gratitude. After years of work, we had succeeded in creating a magical place for our students—it was finally a reality. After the last family hugged us and left, Ron and I swapped stories with Rhonda, one of our teachers who had also been one of my best friends for years. I basked in the glow of the night, giving thanks that I had succeeded in creating a beautiful new life. I had healed from the trauma, and I had learned how to share my story with others. Everything was in the past. Well, almost everything. One weight had continued to linger, even though many years had passed. Sometimes it would bubble up into panic; other times, I would have to swallow my anger until I was able to talk through it and process it with those I trusted.

At the end of that night, I noticed that I had a message on my phone, so I checked my voicemail. My greatest remaining fear had become my reality—it was a message from my tax attorney: "Kim, the IRS has sent me a demand for all of the back taxes plus penalties. They are going to go after you for the full amount since they cannot find your ex-husband. Because these taxes go back several years and there are extreme late penalties, they want $212,000." That's right—not $212.00, but two hundred and twelve thousand dollars.

The room spun, and I crumpled to the floor. Rhonda and Ron immediately slid down on either side of me. Rhonda rubbed my back, and Ron reminded me to breathe. He knew this version of me all too well—he had seen it years ago right when our friendship had begun, and I had finally learned to talk about things.

"Kim, you can do this. You can do anything. Breathe. You have done nothing wrong, and you have the proof. You are going to get through this just like you have overcome everything else." Rhonda nodded in agreement.

How on Earth had this happened? Before I share more, I need to explain a few things — perhaps out of pride and self-preservation; I won't try to pretend otherwise. Keep in mind that I am fifty-four years old. There were no cell phones when this began; there was no social media; I didn't have a home computer for many years. You couldn't ask someone to take a picture to prove where they really were; there were no apps to check. There was no online banking; the only clouds that existed were in the sky. Bills were paid by check and sent through US mail; taxes were done the same way.

You see, X had his own business, and for a period of six years while we were still married, he apparently had made a profitable income (unbeknownst to me), and one-third of that should have gone to Uncle Sam. However, we had struggled financially because he had spent the money on his double life. For several years, I signed tax returns that he presented to me, and I was led to believe that he was placing them in the mail and paying our tax debt. He had not. When I discovered the truth and he realized he could not run from this, he filed several years of returns at once . . . years of returns with my signature on them agreeing to file jointly.

Every night I would lie awake terrified that the IRS would show up at my door and seize everything. The fear and anger were paralyzing. I found a tax attorney who recommended that I start making monthly payments to the IRS of whatever I could possibly afford to show that I was in good faith doing everything I could do to take on this debt, even though X was doing nothing and I was working on a teacher's salary. I began making these payments in October 2002, and I never missed a single one.

Then X disappeared. He left his place of business unlocked and just walked away. He had no job, no bank accounts, and no known address or phone number. To compound matters, tax debt is not like other debt in a divorce. You don't split it fifty-fifty. The IRS will usually seek the money from whoever has the ability to pay. It looked like I was their best option.

What did I do? After doing all I knew to handle the situation, I faithfully mailed money every month, no matter how hard the struggle. It seemed the only sane reaction to this chaotic situation. It was 2007 when I received that fateful call; I had already been sending in payments for five years. Through a long, detailed process, my attorney negotiated a settlement for me. Her advice had been good—my years of payments were noted. The settlement gave me peace; however, I was still required to send in every spare penny I had for yet another five years.

Even when things seem unbearably hopeless, we can choose how to react.

For years I bore the weight of this chapter, but in October 2012, I was finally free. The way that I dealt with this experience was a huge defining factor in the way that I now look at life. I learned that even when things seem unbearably hopeless, we can choose how to react. I could have allowed bitterness and hatred toward X to consume me for twelve years, but it would have destroyed me. I could have tried to ignore the situation in hopes that it would go away, but it would have made matters worse. I could have sought revenge, but instead I sought solutions.

We are all a composite of our life experiences, and those events were a turning point in my life that gave me clarity. Here is the kicker though: in order to move forward, I realized I had to ask myself a terribly difficult question: How did I need to change?

Wait . . . what? He was the only one who should have changed! I was loyal, hardworking, and dedicated. I never betrayed him! I never called him names like the ones he called me! He is the one who did all of the horrific things! The one who ruined us financially! The one who emotionally abused me! I tried so hard!

But deep within me, I knew that if I didn't ask myself this question, I could find myself back in the same relationship—just with a different person. To be clear, if you are being abused, it is not your fault. Ever. I didn't deserve the things that happened to me—no one does. But if I didn't modify my choices, my reactions, and my relationships, I could possibly find myself back in another horrific situation. Acknowledging my weaknesses and making the necessary adjustments made me stronger. It made me better.

Expectations

I realized that I had told myself lies to convince myself it would be okay. I did this to protect myself, but I had to face this truth and modify my path if I wanted my life to change. I was in denial. I was naive. I was an enabler. I had allowed him to manipulate me. I had to accept the truth that people will treat you the way that you allow them to, and I had allowed far too much for far too long. I needed to know my finances. I needed to stop worrying about what others would think. I needed to expect more for myself. I needed to realize my worth, my value. I needed to trust my instincts and the power within me.

> When you settle,
> you are not fine.

And just as we tell ourselves lies about our own behavior, we also tell ourselves lies about others' behavior. We lie to justify another's actions against us.

- He didn't mean it.
- He is going through a lot and is hurting, too.
- I know he loves me — he is just hurting about something himself.
- He will change — I know it.
- It is okay — it really didn't bother me that much.
- I am fine.

When I settled for these lies, I settled for a life that was less than — a life full of pain. When you settle, you are not fine. I was not okay. I would no longer be a victim. I had power to change and to influence my new path forward. So do you. If you are not sure where to start, then be still and ask yourself how you would finish this sentence:

Things would be better if...

Once you have your answers, ask yourself what you can do to make these things a reality. Some things cannot be changed, but some can. Remember, your answer shouldn't be influenced by insecurity, illusions you have created, jealousy for others, selfish wants, or a negative mindset.

For example, here are some healthy responses to *Things would be better if . . .*

- I recognized my value and worth.
- I learned how to take care of myself.
- I educated myself about my finances.
- I focused more on my health.
- I stopped thinking that others' lives are better than mine.
- I focused on my blessings, not my obstacles.
- I treated others better.
- I stopped the same destructive patterns.
- I surrounded myself with people who make me better, not worse.
- I admitted when I am wrong.
- I respected myself and expected others to respect me.
- I learned to be happy for others when good things happen to them.
- I encouraged others.
- I used my heartache to help heal others.
- I focused more on creating healthy relationships.
- I sought to understand others' perspectives.
- I worked on strengthening my mind, body, and spirit.

Some of your answers will be beyond your ability to fix them, so focus on the ones that you can influence by changing your mindset and behaviors. You deserve for things to be better, my friend. You deserve for them to be amazing.

Notes

♪ Do not allow your present circumstances to dictate your current happiness.

♪ If you cannot fix your circumstances, fix your thinking.

♪ Adjust your lens from a negative mindset to a modified mindset.

♪ Allow yourself to feel frustration and pain, but try not to stay there.

♪ Recognize that modifying your mindset can help you face your fears.

♪ Modify your behaviors that bring you pain, frustration, or drama.

♪ Avoid justifying your behaviors and making excuses for the behavior of others.

♪ Determine what would make things better, and work toward making the necessary modifications to make them a reality.

Change Your Tune

♪ Identify times when you have let negative thinking affect your current happiness. How could you have changed the situation by seeing it differently? Practice the modified mindset, and record times that it made a difference for you.

♪ Reflect upon behaviors that you have engaged in that have kept you from achieving your purpose. How can you make changes that will improve your life? Make a list of goals you would like to achieve.

♪ Reflect upon times that you have made excuses for yourself or for another's poor behavior. Write them down and replace them with truths. Stop using these excuses to placate yourself or another.

chapter 3

Identify

Modify

(Amplify)

Unify

Fortify

Battle Cry

When you can take your pain and use it to help heal another's hurting heart, then you AMPLIFY your purpose; you rewrite how the story ends.

2013 As I stand atop a stone wall in Soweto, a township near Johannesburg, South Africa, I watch my students interact and play with the learners at Shalo Mani Primary School. I notice a circle forming around my student Ryan and a bright-eyed charismatic little boy who I later learn is named Sisipho (See-SEE-poh). Sisipho means gift, and he is aptly named. Ryan and the other children are making beats with their mouths as Sisipho raps with delight, all in his native tongue, Xhosa. His language is beautiful — one with clicks and sounds we do not use in the English language, and I am mesmerized as I join the circle, too. When Sisipho finishes, Ryan showers him with high fives and hugs, and everyone cheers.

Later, as I walk into a classroom, another small boy turns around and flashes an epic smile — one that makes my heart skip a beat. He has freckles covering his nose, and when he sees me, he begins to giggle. I have no idea why, but his laugh is so contagious that I, too, giggle with him. He tells me that he is Sisipho's cousin, Phakamani (Pok-uh-MON-ee).

Throughout the week, Sisipho and Phakamani follow us wherever we go. And they are always accompanied by their Zulu friend, Sabelo (Suh-BEL-oh). Sabelo is an artist and a dreamer who carries his prized sketchbook with him because he longs to be an engineer. He shows me his detailed sketches with pride, and I am amazed by his gift.

On one of the final nights of our trip, we gain permission to put the boys on our bus and take them to a beautiful restaurant — one nicer than they had ever experienced. Our tables are set with oval white plates, and we wait with great anticipation for the food that will soon be delivered in large, steaming bowls. The boys engage in lively dialogue with us all until one of my students, Darius, asks, "Sisipho, what happens after high school?" Sisipho's eyes suddenly pool with enormous tears as he swallows hard and puts his head down.

A massive droplet falls upon his plate, and tears of my own start to form. His animated smile is gone, and he hangs his head in silence. Darius looks mortified, and I give him a slight nod to let him know it is okay — he hasn't done anything wrong. However, Sisipho's pain is evident. He doesn't answer Darius because there is no answer. There is no scholarship, no financial aid, no job, no resources. Yet this child, this precious gift, has the same hopes and dreams of every child. An ache washes over me, enveloping me with sadness. I want him to receive an education; I want to help somehow, but I do not know what to do. I am overwhelmed.

Then a small spark begins to ignite from deep within me. I am hesitant to acknowledge it, for I do not have the time, the talents, the resources, the knowledge . . . yet it does not go away. I feel led to act, but if I respond, I know that some will not understand. I try to push it away and dismiss it as my emotions playing tricks on me. But night after night, the feeling grows stronger. I know that I am called to follow my instincts.

oweto is a place of contrasts—poor in resources but rich in love. Teachers often have as many as fifty students in class who are eager to learn but who are denied access to knowledge and supplies. Classrooms lack desks, chairs, textbooks, technology, pencils, paper, and even chalk. Apartheid ended in 1994, yet its effects still permeate the day-to-day lives of the beautiful people who live in Soweto. Many families live in shacks or suffer from deplorable living conditions; many are hungry. And so it is Soweto that our school chooses to visit every year. We have forged bonds with the adults and children alike, and when we arrive, the township is abuzz with excitement because their friends from America have returned with a new class of students bringing supplies for the schools and orphanages. Before our trip, our students spend an entire year fundraising for the children of Soweto—we teach our students the importance of giving to, supporting, and uplifting others. I have been blessed to visit schools on six of the seven continents, yet I have returned to Soweto ten times. It holds a piece of my heart.

The story of the events leading up to our boys' adoptions could be a whole book in itself, but it is not my book to write; it is theirs. My daughter is now a grown woman—one who urged me to write our backstory. However, my sons deserve to be the ones to tell the entirety of their experiences when they become adults and choose to do so. It is a story filled with pain and beauty, heartache and miracles.

On June 12, 2014, our beloved boys arrived at the Hartsfield–Jackson Atlanta International Airport with one backpack shared among them. Its contents included Sabelo's prized sketchbook, a belt, and pajamas. Our life as a family had begun. My sons speak five languages—Zulu, Xhosa, Sotho, Afrikaans, and English. However, when they arrived at age twelve, they could not add or multiply; Sisipho could not read. If you ever doubt the impact that educators can make, you must know that the teachers at RCA poured into my sons, supported them, and taught them magnificently. Imagine entering a seventh-grade social studies class at a rigorous school when you do not know what a state is, a country is, or the Civil Rights Movement was. My boys had no prior knowledge to build upon, making learning even more difficult, yet their brilliant minds were like sponges when given the educational opportunities that every child deserves. Each night, Scotty and I would sit at the table for four to five hours with the boys, teaching them everything they had never learned. They craved knowledge and answers, and their joy for learning fueled us until we collapsed into bed each night.

Phakamani (top left)
Sabelo (top right)
Sisipho (left)

My sons are my very heartbeat — they have blessed Scotty, Madison, and me beyond measure — but it has been a complicated journey. I am a fifty-four-year-old white woman from suburbia who has three African sons. I still cringe whenever someone approaches me and says, "OMG! You have adopted those boys? You are just like Angelina Jolie!" The concept of white saviorism is an issue in our society — it manifests itself when white people assume that we are the only "hope" to save children of color from poverty or destruction, that somehow we know what people of color need more than they know themselves. This is one of the reasons that RCA goes back to the same places in Soweto year after year to learn and provide what the people actually ask for, not what we assume they need. They know far better than we do what solutions will be truly helpful. We do not want to be among those who pop in once, snap photos for our social media feeds to impress people, and then forever disappear without doing the real work. It is also the reason why Ron and I, two white cofounders, have been intentional about hiring a diverse staff who can share truths with us, empowering us to be better educators for our students.

I am certain that some have seen my family and have drawn such conclusions about us, and I understand why some express concern when they do not fully know me, my heart, the details of our story, and the people who pour into our family. After all, what do I know about raising strong black young men? And how do I keep their magnificent African culture alive? These are valid questions to ask. It has been imperative to surround our family with people who can help me raise my sons—people of color with knowledge and experiences that I can never fully comprehend, people who educate me as I constantly seek to understand. I am blessed to be part of an incredibly

Sabelo received his RCA jacket for working so hard

diverse staff as well — one where we engage in frequent conversations about race, ethnicity, culture, and differences; one where we constantly seek love, understanding, and insight.

There were nights, especially at the beginning, when I was completely overwhelmed from the sheer exhaustion of it all; there were days when my eyes would burn from lack of sleep. And we have encountered red tape at every turn. Keep in mind that I am also an administrator, classroom teacher, and professional development trainer — I have numerous jobs in addition to that of wife and mother. But as with all parents, the incomprehensible joy that my children give my life outweighs every bit of struggle. My sons have taught me that every child learns differently, loves differently, and heals differently. They have not only had a profound impact upon me, but the ripple effect of their lives has had an impact upon countless others beyond our family. Their lives have amplified my purpose.

The boys' second day in the United States

> When you give your love and support
> to the lives of others, it is exponentially
> magnified beyond comprehension.

When we serve others, we seek to make a change in their lives. However, it is we who are actually changed the most. By loving my sons and providing a life for them, my life has been enriched beyond measure. And it's not just my life. My sons have had an extensive impact on our family, friends, coworkers, and all whom they have touched with their radiant light. The same is true with you. When you give your love and support to the lives of others, it is exponentially magnified beyond comprehension.

Purpose

When you are happy, helping others fuels the soul. And when you feel the depths of despair, serving others is a cleansing balm for your wounds. Uplifting others gives you a purpose, power, and passion for life, even when you feel alone, afraid, overworked, or overwhelmed. As a wise preacher once said, "There is a point to my life, and I am not it."

When you shift your focus to someone else, amazing things start to occur. You start to see beyond your pain, and you realize that you have a purpose bigger than yourself. Here is the amazing reality: whenever you help one person, you do not only help that person. You also help that person's family, friends, employees, colleagues, neighbors, community members — everyone with whom the recipient of your good deeds interacts has been affected. You have amplified your purpose in immeasurable ways.

It isn't just in our dark hours that we should focus upon others; every day is filled with divine appointments — opportunities to have an impact that amplifies our relationships, reach, and reasons for being. We can listen, uplift, support, and assist. We can pour into, seek understanding, and provide insight. Sometimes you will know your impact, but often you will have no idea. Other times, things will work out differently than you expected, but your good deeds will not have been done in vain.

I have been blessed to teach many beautiful children and know many extraordinary families, but the Copeland family was one that captured my heart from the very beginning. I had the pleasure of teaching both Jacobi and Maya, two siblings whose love for writing was accompanied by incredible creativity and depth of character. Tatanisha and Carlos Copeland are loving, kind parents who often go above and beyond to show appreciation for others. For example, one time I was at the Atlanta airport and posted that my flight had been delayed three times due to weather. Carlos, who was a bag handler at the time, appeared at my gate with a piece of red velvet cake and a Diet Coke just to make my night better. Who does that? Carlos Copeland, that's who.

When I learned that Carlos was in advanced stages of kidney disease, I didn't want to accept it. At the time, I didn't fully understand how the progression of his illness was taking its toll upon the whole family. I just knew that they were one of the most loving, bonded families I had ever known, and Jacobi and Maya were sad, and Carlos was losing a lot of weight. Yet despite this, Tatanisha was still always one to check on me, reach out to me, and support me and our other staff members. I then heard Carlos was looking for a kidney donor. That should be easy, right? Wrong. His family was not a match, and although some others had considered donating a kidney, none were able to do so.

So, there I sat in church one Sunday, and I could think of nothing else but the Copelands. A feeling overcame me, and I knew that I needed to offer Carlos my kidney. I cannot explain it other than to tell you that I was completely certain. Peace washed over me. After church I told my husband, and he said, "Of course, honey, if you feel led to do so."

At carpool the following day, I asked Tatanisha to come inside, and I told her that I wanted to donate my kidney to her husband. She held me tightly, and then we sat hand in hand as she told me how to start the process. After the first initial tests, I learned that my kidney was a match. Was I shocked? Nope. I felt like I had known it all along.

For most of the following year, I visited a series of doctors. I was poked and prodded. I had psychiatric testing to see if I could handle the emotional ramifications and financial screening to see if I could take off of work. I was placed on treadmills with electrodes to test my physical condition. I was given a colonoscopy. Things were moving full speed ahead. And then they weren't. Tests came back saying I had exceptionally high levels of calcium, causing hypercalcemia. I know—calcium sounds like it would be a good thing, but too much is not. I was placed on a regimen of vitamin D supplements to get my calcium levels in check; I made numerous visits to an endocrinologist. It made no sense—I felt absolutely fine, but the kidney specialists kept saying I couldn't be cleared for donation just yet. And all the while, Carlos grew sicker. I peed in container after container to keep retesting my levels, but they were not good. (Not any container—these were half gallon jugs that had to be filled.) I even took my urine jug in a cooler on a road trip to one of my speeches, just to stay on track. I was bound and determined to fix what I couldn't see or even control—it was literally a matter of life or death. Finally, in February 2017, I was given an answer: a resounding no. I had taken a final test that indicated I am at high risk for kidney stones, and I guess if you have only one kidney, this is not a good thing. I know—as you read this, you are completely disappointed. You wanted the happy ending after reading all of that. Imagine how we felt.

I was devastated. I was confused. I knew I was supposed to give Carlos my kidney—I was sure of it! I was a perfect match! Why would God allow me to have peace and to go through several months of tests, only to be told I couldn't do it? I couldn't bear to tell Carlos, either. I had to tell Tatanisha so she could tell him in her own gentle, beautiful way, but telling her broke my heart.

Sometimes God orchestrates our lives better than we can orchestrate them ourselves. After I was given my final no, Ron posted a picture of the Copelands on Facebook and shared that they were looking for a kidney. Staci Erickson, a teacher who had visited RCA but had never even met the Copelands, responded to the post and messaged Tatanisha. She had the same overwhelming calling to help, but Staci was spot on. She was a match. She donated her kidney to Carlos, a man she had never met before, and saved his life. Beautiful. She is an angel.

So, it all worked out, and there was a happy ending after all. But I must admit, I was confused. How had I misunderstood my instincts? Especially with something so serious? It was several months later when it all came together. Tatanisha and Carlos invited Scotty and me to a celebratory dinner after Carlos was back on the road to recovery. I shared that I still felt so bad about putting them through months of waiting, all for naught.

Carlos said, "Kim, you didn't give me a kidney. You gave me hope."

Tatanisha added, "Kim, Carlos tried to be so strong—we all did—but during those months, the hope that you might be the one kept us going in our darkest hours. You were our light."

So, there you have it. Sometimes you may not be the solution, the answer, the fix. But if you are willing to give freely of yourself, you might just be the hope, the light, the strength, the support that sustains and soothes another until things get better. And that can be enough. Just making yourself accessible is a gift in itself, not only to the recipient, but to your soul as well.

Healing

It was Christmas Eve, and after opening some of our gifts, Scotty, my children, and I all snuggled on the sectional watching television. Our bellies protruded from our pajamas after our magnificent feast, and overwhelming warmth, joy, and gratitude swelled within me.

I picked up my phone to take a photo of the flickering lights on the Christmas tree when I noticed a new email—one that simply said "Please help" in the subject line. I opened it to read a letter from a woman I didn't know, but who had heard me tell parts of my story at a speech several months before. As I read her words, my heart ached for her—it was as if I could feel her fingers trembling as she typed; I could imagine the tears rolling down her cheeks. You see, just hours before, she had found a text message, then a receipt, after which her world had fallen apart. I knew that storyline all too well. Her husband had betrayed her, and she felt alone, scared, angry, broken, and devastated. She didn't have words yet—she didn't know whom she could trust, whom she should tell. Therefore, she reached out to me, a stranger whose contact information she found on our school website. I was glad she did.

After exchanging a few emails, I asked her if she would like to talk. She said she would, so I called her. Much of the next hour was spent just listening and supporting this woman. She did not know me well, but I wanted her to know that she wasn't alone, especially on Christmas Eve. She was able to muster the strength to call a good friend after we hung up — one who could be there with her in the days ahead. Almost one year later, she reached back out to me to let me know that she and her husband were working it out. It was slow and difficult, but she felt like they really had a shot at it. I was so happy to hear the hope in her words.

Did I mind stepping away from my family and talking to a stranger for an hour on Christmas Eve? My family is my everything, but I was grateful to be chosen for the task, and I considered it to be the best of Christmas gifts.

When you can take your pain and use it to help heal another's hurting heart, then you amplify your purpose; you rewrite how the story ends. You know that it didn't happen in vain. Your thinking is modified, and a new reality replaces the old: you are better and stronger for having experienced it. Do not be ashamed or embarrassed by your life's struggles. Sharing your story does not make you weak — it makes you strong. I am not suggesting that you go on Facebook every night and share all your business and drama; this is just attention seeking. But when you share your story in the appropriate context, it can encourage and empower; it can help others rewrite their chapters, too.

When I was in my darkest hours, I would push down my hurt and tuck it away into a little box that held pain, sorrow, embarrassment, anger, fear, and denial. This was my survival mechanism, and it enabled me to keep functioning. But if you continue to tuck things into your box without emptying it, eventually the box will break, and its contents will seep out into your life in other ways. The suppressed emotions can be misdirected, magnified, and misinterpreted. They can hurt other relationships, sabotage future success, and divert you from your true purpose.

When I was betrayed, I told no one — not another living soul. I am very social — I have supportive friends and family, but I just couldn't find the strength to talk about it. Some of you have been there. I tucked that pain away like it was something to be ashamed of — like I was somehow less than. I didn't even know how to find the words to explain it to anyone. When I finally decided to take control and start unpacking my truth, I grew stronger than ever before. By experiencing and sharing my pain, I amplified my empathy.

I want the same for you. If your box is full, take time to empty it, but do it slowly and gently at first. Be kind to yourself. Unpack it by sharing your story with someone you trust — it might even need to be a professional counselor or therapist. But you must find a way to do it. There is no shame in unpacking . . . it is empowering. You are the one taking back control.

For example, as you can imagine, my experiences gave me major trust issues. If I didn't unpack those feelings, I would have never been able to freely entrust my heart to my beloved husband, Scotty, and I never would have been able to be in a healthy relationship with him. For me, it required some counseling to get to the point where I could fully release my heart. The interesting revelation for me was that I had to learn to trust myself and my judgment before I could learn to trust others. I felt like I had let myself down by allowing myself to be betrayed. Once I learned to trust myself, I was better able to trust my Scotty fully and completely.

Once you have unpacked that box, you are free — free of the weight, free of the burden, and free to speak about your pain. Once the pain has been processed, you will be able to use it to help others who are enduring heartache of their own. When I reflect upon my journey, I know that the challenges in my life made me a more empathetic and understanding person. If my life had been without pain, I might not have the same capacity for compassion that I now possess. My burdens made me better. It has been said that "hurt people hurt people," but I believe that hurt people can also help heal people in some of the most heartfelt ways of all.

Significance

By nature, I am a very type-A personality. In my younger years, I was hyper-focused on achievements, and if I failed, I was devastated. I thought that somehow this mindset would determine my happiness and success; I would be validated. But awards are just objects that gather dust on a shelf unless you use them as a platform for your voice. There are so many who deserve recognition and do not receive it; therefore, if you do, it is your duty to be a representative for all who have not been granted the same opportunities. I am grateful for the recognition I have received, but only because it has helped me use my voice to help teachers and students. Stockpiling trophies and certificates on a shelf will not create happiness.

There came a point in my life where I re-evaluated everything, and I asked myself, *Kim, why do you do the things you do?* When I was honest with myself, I didn't like all of the answers. Yes, I have always been motivated by my desire to help children; I am wired to love them with my whole being. But there was a part of me who sought achievements in a quest for perfection. Perfection is boring, overrated, and unattainable. The quest for perfection is exhausting and even destructive at times.

Most of us spend our days seeking to achieve, but in the wee hours when we lie awake, it is significance that our hearts truly desire. We long to know that our lives count for something; that they matter. We hope that we have made an impact that has affected others in exponential ways. So, I shifted my focus. No longer would I seek achievements; I would seek significance. Achievements are about getting something, but significance is about *being* something. When you seek significance, the achievements still happen, but when they don't — like when a door closes that you thought would be open, or when you get a no that you thought would be a yes, or when that person leaves whom you thought would always stay — it still hurts. It hurts so badly. But you are able to understand that perhaps that door closed so that you can go through another one instead — a door that will have a bigger and better impact upon the lives of others.

Achievements are about getting something, but significance is about BEING something.

When you seek significance, you focus on how you amplify your reach to impact, empower, and uplift others. You amplify your purpose. It is not about you. You are not thinking about yourself or about getting credit for doing good; you are seeking to make an exponential difference in this world.

Last winter, my father's health battles required us to move him into a full-time care facility, and cleaning out his home was an overwhelming task for my two older brothers and me. One by one, we sorted through a lifetime of photos, keepsakes, mementos, and collectibles. Some items we kept, some we sold, and others we gave away. It was both painful and enlightening to realize that all of my parents' possessions were relegated to boxes in a garage, waiting to be hauled away. However, there were many things that we clung to, not for their material value but rather for what they represented to us. My parents' wedding album, my father's baby book from 1935, and our pictures with Santa were carefully distributed among us. The Hummels? No one cared. The worn-out chair that my mother used to rock us to sleep was kept, but we sold the newer dining room set for close to nothing. For us, it was the items that held cherished moments and had memories attached to them that had significance. My fathers' work trophies? We put them in a box in my brother's basement because we didn't know where else to put them. But the sweatshirt that still smells like my daddy? I kept it to wrap it around myself like a hug.

As you can imagine, the whole exercise was hard for Daddy, and I needed him to know that, although his things did not matter to us, his story did. Our love for him had nothing to do with his dining room table. To this day, I regret the questions I never asked my mother, and I long to hear recordings of her voice. I can still remember it vividly, but I fear that as I grow older, the sound of it will fade away. Who was my mother before she was my mother? What were her hopes and dreams? What was she proud of? What was her biggest regret? If I had asked my mother more questions, perhaps she would have known how significant she truly was. I decided that I couldn't make the same mistake with Daddy, so Sisipho helped me create a cherished series of videos.

Over the course of several weeks, Sisipho recorded me interviewing my father. We talked about his childhood, his favorite toys, his friends, the mischief he created, and his academic prowess. I learned about his first kiss, his paper route, and his love for his cousins. I now know how he met my mother, his service in the navy, his leadership, and how he helped others throughout his career. As he answered all of my questions, his eyes sparkled and shone, tearing up at times. By recounting his life's journey, he realized that he has done great good in this world; he has made a significant impact — especially on me.

To be of significance, we must remember to identify our worth and our gifts so we can use them to amplify our purpose — one that will make a difference in the lives of others. What do you care about? What are you passionate about? What are you angry about? When you lie in bed at night, what keeps you awake? The tiniest tugs within your heart are directing you where to

To be of significance, we must remember to identify our worth and our gifts so we can use them to amplify our purpose — one that will make a difference in the lives of others.

start. For me, it has always been about children. Then I became passionate about inequities in education.

Our school exists to amplify our impact upon students everywhere. When Ron and I cofounded RCA, we had a vision to affect as many children's lives as possible, even those who did not go to our school each day. How could we possibly do that? Through teachers. We realized that if we could support teachers and give them tools for success, we would be helping students in their classrooms. We decided to create a place that was not only a school for our precious students; it would also be a place where we provided professional development, motivation, inspiration, and validation for educators. We would support them and help them, and by doing so, we would be able to help our students who could not afford to pay tuition. As I write this, tens of thousands of educators have come to our school to learn our methods. These teachers will impact the lives of millions during the span of their careers. As a non-profit, 100 percent of the proceeds from our professional development days go to support student scholarships and school programs. By supporting other teachers, we are uplifting RCA students and other students around the globe as well. It is my life's calling. It is my response to seeking significance.

Kindness

To be clear, you don't have to adopt three children, donate a kidney, or start a school to have significance! Sometimes it is the smallest of gestures that have a lasting impact. In the fall of 1982, I was a proud member of the Wheeler High School drill team; I wore my white leather boots, navy satin vest, and polyester short-shorts with pride. Our drill team sponsor was also

Ron and me
(photo by J. Amezqua)

my favorite English teacher, Nancy Quattlebaum. Oh, how I loved her — she was strict, yet kind; challenging, yet supportive. When she looked at me, I felt like she truly saw me. She taught me to love writing; she also taught me to love myself.

One night at practice, I stood in formation under the glow of the stadium lights, tears pooling in my eyes. To be honest, I don't remember why. I remember the feeling, though — I was sad, exhausted, overwhelmed, and filled with anxiety. I am sure it was typical teen drama, but at the time it seemed major. I was hurting.

I met eyes with Ms. Quattlebaum, and while the band played on, she approached me, took my hand, and pulled me over to a bench. She lightly patted my back with one hand as she continued to hold my hand with the other. "Do you need a moment?" she said in the gentlest of voices.

"Yes," I said. Her kindness made me cry harder, but I felt so comforted by her actions, her concern. Everything else just faded away. In that moment, it was just me and her, and that was what I needed. I remember trying to explain why I was upset, but I had no words. So, we sat on the sidelines under the glow of the lights for as long as I needed. The anxiety washed away, and calm overtook me. Finally, I looked her in the eyes and said, "Thank you, Ms. Quattlebaum. I feel so much better now." I gave her a hug and returned to the formation.

When I entered college, Ms. Quattlebaum asked me to be part of a mentoring program she had created for young girls. She taught me how to make other young girls feel validated, just as she had done with me. Ms. Quattlebaum's beautiful life was short—she passed away while still in her thirties—but her purpose was magnified through me and all of the students she loved and poured into in the most magnificent ways. Because of that one simple moment with Ms. Quattlebaum, I have spent thirty-three years as an educator doing my darndest to see my students in the same way she saw me struggling under those stadium lights—to notice, to stop, to take time, to listen, to just be with them. Sometimes, no words are needed. Sometimes, just being there is what makes a difference. I have taught thousands of students in my lifetime, and that moment with Ms. Quattlebaum indirectly affected each and every one of the students I have reached.

Sometimes, my students have been affected when I didn't even know they were paying attention, for you never know who is watching or listening. Several years ago, I was fortunate to take our seventh-grade students on a trip to London. Our day had been filled with sightseeing tours, and before we knew it, we were late for dinner. We had tickets for a play that evening, and we wanted to be there on time. Therefore, Ron, the other chaperones, and I decided to divide and conquer. We went to a local food court, and each of us took a handful of kids. Yes, we should have been dining on fish and chips, but I found myself in line at McDonald's with my group, desperate to get our food and eat it all within fifteen minutes. There were only two people in line in front of us, but there was also only one person behind the counter. As soon as I studied him in action, I knew we were doomed. He moved so very slowly, almost as if he were on heavy medication. His shoulders slumped as he trod back and forth, back and forth, picking up orders and filling drinks.

We finally placed our order with only ten minutes remaining. Then I watched him pull out our seven paper cups and walk back and forth, back and forth to fill them — one at a time. I admit it, I wanted to scream, "For the love of God, please try to hurry!" But instead, I took a deep breath and took into consideration that he had a story and I had no idea was it was to be in his position. He was obviously sad, he was alone, and he might have been doing the very best he could. So, instead, I said, "Sir, it looks like you have your hands full and there is only one of you. How can I help? Can I bring the rest of the cups over to you?" He shrugged and nodded, and I grabbed all of the paper cups and brought them to the opposite side of the counter where he stood at the soda machines. I passed out the drinks, and I even helped him with the drinks for the party behind ours as we waited on our food. He smiled and thanked me as we briskly departed. We wolfed down our dinner as we walked, making it to our show just in time.

I never gave that experience a second thought until a full year later when Tyler, one of my students, handed me a thank-you note that expressed her gratitude for being in my class. Her words were beautifully written, but one part absolutely leapt off of the page:

> I will always remember many things about your class, but most of all, I will remember the time we were in the food court in London. We were all so frustrated, but you treated the man behind the counter with kindness. You offered to help him, and you did it without making him feel like he was doing a bad job. I will always remember how you handled that situation. You are the kind of woman I want to become one day.

I had many incredible experiences with Tyler, yet the one that meant the most to her took me by surprise. It helped me realize that all good, kind actions — even the simplest ones — are amplified when we do them for others. If we all could be kinder, gentler, and more patient, it would have a ripple effect that would transform this world. Our days are filled with opportunities to serve and support others, and when we do so with a willing heart, it is we who are changed. In my book *Talk to Me*, I share the power of extraordinary acts of kindness — doing wonderful things for someone without talking about

> # All good, kind actions —
> ## even the simplest ones — are amplified
> ## when we do them for others.

it, posting it, or seeking credit for it. When you are feeling sorrow or heartache, shift your focus to someone who is in need. How can you help them? In doing so, it will help you heal; you will realize that the greatest kind of power is when we empower others.

Sometimes it is the simplest things that make the biggest difference. Write someone a note, help them clean their room, grade their papers. Watch someone's kids, gift them with a small token of appreciation. Give food to the hungry, give time to the lonely. Listen to someone who just needs an ear. Do not worry if you receive thanks — if you focus on getting credit, then you will sometimes be disappointed. Rather, focus on the giving rather than the getting. Do not tell everyone you did it. Let it be your own secret. I promise you that your soul will be rewarded immeasurably.

Legacy

On the divine day that I first met my sons, it was Ryan Marshall who brought us all together. Ryan was a joyful child whose heart was pure and good. When he was in the fifth grade, Ron and I heard that one of our fifth graders had been heard cussing. We didn't know who it was, so we called a class meeting. We talked about the importance of the words we choose and explained that cussing simply would not be tolerated. Ron then said, "Raise your hand if you have been cussing." Ryan put his head down, slumped his shoulders, and raised his hand. Ron said, "Ryan, I am shocked! You cussed?"

Ryan replied, "Mr. Clark, when I walked into school the other day, I stubbed my toe and it hurt really bad. I didn't say it out loud, but I cussed in my head and I know that is just as bad."

I had to swallow my giggle.

Ryan was also a truly gifted musician — he wrote songs, mixed them, made videos for them, sang them, and rapped them. His lyrics had depth, and we were amazed at what he was able to create using nothing more than a little phone. Academically, Ryan didn't have the same drive as he had with his music, although we all adored having him in class. When he smiled with his huge dimples, he lit up the room.

So, when Ryan befriended my son Sisipho on a playground in Soweto, their bond was instantaneous. Ryan loved Sisipho, and he was devastated when he had to leave him behind. When Ryan returned to the States, he was transformed academically — he said he would never take his education for granted again, and he worked hard in every subject and asked Ron to tutor him to make him even stronger.

When my boys arrived here, we surprised Ryan, and Sisipho and Ryan's reunion took my breath away. Through tears of joy, Ryan told Sisipho that he had affected his life and that he had inspired him to do more. He said, "I am better because of you." Their friendship had been divinely arranged.

Ryan with Sisipho
in Soweto

Nine months after my sons moved here, I received the call that changed our lives forever. It was Ron. He was at Grady Hospital. He said to come quickly. Ryan had been shot.

I screamed for Scotty and the boys and told them we had to get to the hospital right away. And then my phone rang again — it was Dasia, Ryan's older sister. Dasia had always been like a daughter to me — she has always called me Mama.

"Mama! What is happening? Where is Ryan? No one will answer their phones! Someone said he's hurt. Please help me!" she sobbed. Dasia was three hours away at college, and she had found out through social media.

"Baby, who is with you? Are you alone?" I asked.

"Yes. But who is with Ryan? What happened?" she wailed.

"I don't know, sweetie. I am trying to find out. I am leaving for Grady now," I said.

Scotty, who had heard the whole conversation on speaker phone said, "Dasia, text me your address. I am driving to get you now. I will be there in three hours."

I nodded in gratitude, and Scotty kissed me, grabbed his keys, and ran out the door. As soon as he was on the road, he called Junior Bernadin, our dean of students, who called a fraternity brother who lived where Dasia did — he went to pick her up to get her to Atlanta even faster. Scotty, however, continued the three-hour drive to pick up Dasia's boyfriend so that he could be there to support her in the days ahead.

Meanwhile, I frantically loaded my sons into the car and headed to Grady, questions spinning through my head. *How? Why?* When we arrived, the waiting room was overflowing, but through my tears I spotted Ron across the room. He rushed over to me and held me.

"Kim, he just passed," he whispered, his voice catching. I began to shake.

Someone came over to us and asked Ron and me if we would like to say goodbye. I cannot remember who it was because I was in shock, but I do remember Ron guiding me down a long, white hallway and into a room where our precious Ryan lay peacefully.

We went to opposite sides of the bed and each placed our hands upon him. I prayed, but I kept my eyes open the whole time because I wanted to forever remember every contour of his sweet face . . . I longed to see his dimples one last time.

The events that followed are a blur . . . my consciousness felt detached from my physical self, and when I tried to move, it seemed like a dream where your body wants to run but your legs cannot. Emotions swirled from one to the next—despair, grief, dismay, anger. *Sisipho! Would he be okay?* I realized that I had to pull it together to comfort him, my other sons, and my students who loved this child so deeply.

We later learned that a carjacker had been in Ryan's front yard trying to steal a car from Ryan's stepfather. Ryan saw this happening through the window and yelled for his mother. She flung the front door open right as the gunman turned the gun toward her. Ryan leapt in front of his mother, taking the bullet for her and saving her life. He was a hero.

Ryan is no longer with us physically, but his legacy lives on and its exponential reach is unlimited. If it were not for Ryan, I would not have met Sisipho and my other sons—Ryan's love gave me my family and changed our lives. Those who knew Ryan still listen to his music—another gift that he left behind. In April 2020, we opened the Ryan Marshall Performing Arts Center on the Ron Clark Academy campus, a state-of-the-art performing arts facility that will forever celebrate the life, love, laughter, and music that Ryan shared with us all.

At RCA's ten-year anniversary, my son Sisipho was asked to speak about Ryan to a crowd of a thousand guests, including Oprah Winfrey. As I watched my son command the stage and share a part of their story, tears of gratitude streamed down my face. Here is an excerpt from his speech:

> My name is Sisipho, and I am from Soweto, South Africa. Soweto is a place filled with beautiful and loving people, but the remnants of apartheid also make it a place that is filled with poverty and broken dreams. I was living in a garage in Soweto the year that my life changed. It was 2013. It was the year that I met Ryan Marshall.
>
> Ryan and his classmates from RCA came to Soweto and visited my school, Shalo Mani Primary School. Our

Every time we help another, love another,
serve another, or see another,
we make music. We create moments
that transcend the present and
spill into the future.

school lacked books, technology, and other basic resources, and the students from RCA came to bring us supplies.

Ryan and I made a special bond immediately. Ryan had this bright light about him, and everyone was drawn to him. Yet he noticed me, a goofy little boy from South Africa. When the RCA students left, I cried because I felt like a part of my heart left when Ryan did. I prayed that one day I would be able to see him again.

Not only did Ryan change my life; he also saved my life. You see, because Ryan noticed me, others did as well. Because of Ryan, my brothers—Phakamani and Sabelo—and I were given scholarships to attend RCA. But the miracle didn't stop there. Mr. and Mrs. Bearden adopted my brothers and me . . . and Mr. and Mrs. Bearden are now my mom and dad, and we are now one big, beautiful family. My whole life has changed, and the opportunities I have before me are because of Ryan's love for me.

But Ryan did not only save my life. He saved his mother's life as well. After I moved to America, Ryan was tragically shot and killed while blocking a bullet from hitting his mother. She had opened the door to find a carjacker in her front yard, and the carjacker turned the gun on her. His life came to a tragic end doing what he always did—caring for someone else.

Ryan was loving, kind, and crazy talented. His ability to make music moved everyone who heard it. When I moved to America, I thought that I would be able to spend the rest of my life with Ryan, and it ripped my heart out when he passed. But I will live my life with passion and joy and love to honor him. I am so happy to know that the Ryan Marshall Performing Arts Center will be a place filled with music and the memory of my dear friend.

He will live in the hearts of us all forever.

That, dear friend, is a life of impact. A life amplified. And you, too, can live such a life. You don't have to be able to sing or make music the way that Ryan could. You see, every time we help another, love another, serve another, or see another, we make music. We create moments that transcend the present and spill into the future. Our joined heartbeats play a song that empowers others to do more, be more, love more, and live more. You need only to be willing to share your time, your talents, your heart. Sometimes, you need to just listen; other times you need to speak life into someone. But in doing so, make no mistake — you are expanding and amplifying your purpose. Isn't that truly what we all need to know? When we feel broken down, beaten down, alone, or afraid, we need to know that our lives matter . . . and they do. Oh, how *you* do, my friend. The more you give of yourself, the more you gain of yourself. Your significance echoes and quakes, moves and shakes all who are affected by you.

Notes

♪ Serving others is a cleansing balm that heals.
♪ When we define our purpose, we begin to find our voice.

♪ When we assist others, our purpose is amplified.

♪ Every day is filled with divine appointments where we can uplift and support others.

♪ By giving freely of yourself, you can provide hope, light, and strength.

♪ Significance is not about getting something; it is about being something.

♪ Even the smallest gestures can still have a profound impact.

♪ Every time we help, serve, love, and see others, we leave a legacy.

Change Your Tune

♪ Identify ways that you can participate in serving, helping, or uplifting others. Take advantage of these opportunities without expecting anything in return. Some of these acts of kindness can be in the moment; others can be planned. Reflect upon each experience.

♪ Reflect upon ways that you can seek a life of significance. What is important to you? How can you live your life in such a way that you are moving toward significance?

chapter **4**

Identify

Modify

Amplify

(Unify)

Fortify

Battle Cry

*We are designed to be social creatures —
to UNIFY ourselves with others.
When we are unified, we are stronger,
healthier, and better able to navigate
the twists and turns of life.*

2016 *It has been difficult to sell this beloved place; it has been on the market for weeks. If others could only understand the joy that flourished within these walls, surely they would see its beauty. It has been our beloved home — a place where we have grown into a family. I want — I need — others to understand. I pour my feelings into a poem, print it on thin parchment paper, and place it on the kitchen counter in hopes that my words will adequately explain the love that abounds here.*

If these walls could talk,
they would tell you how the morning sunlight streams through
*   the windows,*
casting a golden glow onto the floor like a warm quilt.
Music and laughter spill out of children's rooms,
filling the house with joy.
It was in this place that two parents grew to know their three adopted sons
and to love them beyond comprehension.
This house is filled with memories of potluck suppers,
gatherings with friends, competitive board games, family movie nights,
skateboards, basketballs, skinned knees, crocodile tears, and bear hugs.
These walls would share memories of loved ones visiting often
to relax and reconnect through front porch chats and back porch
*   barbecues—*
all who entered were embraced like family.
A spirit of love, peace, and joy permeates this space;
it overflows with goodness and gratitude.
And while those who lived here are so very sad to leave,
they are grateful for the chance to bequeath this sanctuary to others
who will create their own memories
by loving deeply and living life well.
For you see, this is no ordinary house—
it is truly a home.

Years before, when Madison and I spent all those nights in her room, I dreamed about the home I would create one day. It would be a sanctuary, a place of comfort where friends and loved ones would congregate and celebrate. In my book *Talk to Me*, I shared how I moved out of my former home and gave away almost everything inside of it. It was a cleansing experience for me. After I sold that house, I could not wait to find a new place—I didn't really care what it looked like. Madison, now grown, was living a wonderful life on her own, and Scotty and I moved to a simple, tiny, two-bedroom rental home closer to RCA. My tax debt was finally paid, and I was able to start saving for the first time. I had never been happier. We loved that little house so much, but it was difficult to have people over in such a tight space. The living room was two arms' lengths across, making it comical to have more than four people in the space at once.

When we had finally saved enough for a minimal down payment, I noticed a house around the corner with a For Sale sign. It was actually an odd house — long and narrow with numerous windows. However, I loved our neighborhood very much, so I made a mental note of the address and looked it up online. It was over our maximum budget, making it impossible to even consider.

Two months later, Scotty and I sat on the patio of a neighborhood restaurant discussing our housing options. Should we stay put or try to buy a home with a little more space? We would have to move farther away for a bigger place. Should we see if we could buy our beloved rental house and try to add a room to it in the future? My phone dinged, and I looked to see who had sent a text.

It wasn't a person — it was the real estate website that had sent an alert: the house list price had been dropped . . . by thousands of dollars, putting it within our budget. There was an open house scheduled for the following day, and I told Scotty I just had to go. We drove by it after dinner and he said, "This house? It is long and skinny and looks kinda odd, honey." He just laughed, though, and told me to enjoy the open house — he had to coach a game and couldn't join me.

The next day I walked through the front door and immediately noticed the sunlight that shone through every window. Peace washed over me. I was home. The house had issues and needed repairs. It had been inhabited by college students for years, and they had left it with everything from dart holes to broken windowsills. The house had been renovated several times to create a makeshift dormitory — bedroom, bathroom, bedroom, bathroom. But I knew I was home.

When Scotty came home that night, I couldn't stop talking about the place. "Scotty, it is bigger than we want, and it needs work, but we can use it to have students over, friends over . . . we can let people stay there who need a place to go. We can fix it up ourselves! It will be so fun! Can you please go look at it?"

The next day, Scotty met with the realtor while I was at school. I bombarded him with questions when he came through the door that evening. "What do you think? Do you like it? Do you see its potential? We can use it to help people! We can make it really nice!"

"Kim, the carpet is so nasty that I know we will have to replace it all. The upstairs ceiling has water damage. It needs a ton of work. But there is something about it. Maybe we can negotiate a lower price so we can get the work done."

"You mean you are okay with us buying it?" I asked.

"Well, if we can get a deal, then of course," he replied.

We moved into our home over Thanksgiving break, and I went from room to room, praying blessings over every space. We had no furniture for the upstairs dormitory-like bedrooms, but we didn't need it. I planned to have an alumni girls' slumber party as soon as we replaced the carpets, and they would love the open floor space. The house would be a place where I could invite many to enjoy time together.

We laughed because we were so happy in what could best be described as a miniature frat house. No one could understand why we bought that house without looking at any others and how we knew it was the place meant for us. Even we couldn't explain it . . . until I walked back through the door six months later after my serendipitous trip to South Africa.

"Scotty, there are three little boys who need us. . . . Could we? Should we? Can they possibly join our family?"

"Of course."

And so, three twelve-year-old boys joined our family and filled every nook and cranny of our home — it was now their home, too.

Every day, a revolving cast of friends, coworkers, students, parents, and loved ones rotated through our home. The boys' future classmates organized meals for us, and for the first two months, RCA parents and students showed up every Sunday with dinners for the week, complete with recipes and instructions so I could make them in the future. My lack of cooking ability had been no secret, and my beloved RCA parents wanted to make sure the boys were well fed so I could focus on all of their other needs.

We were surrounded by the love of people who fueled our souls. I embraced it all and allowed myself to receive it, to accept their help, to let it wash over me. It was transformative for me.

We created beautiful memories in that house, and we stayed there until it was time for our boys to enter high school—we wanted to find a place in a school zone that could best meet their needs. But who on Earth would buy the place? It was a challenge to sell at first—it still had issues. I decided that if someone knew this wasn't just any house, they would love it, too. They only needed to know more about the people who had inhabited it and the memories that had been created there. So, I composed that poem, printed it on parchment, and set it on the kitchen counter in hopes that prospective buyers would read it and understand. They did.

The house was under contract the following week.

Joy
(photo by J. Amezqua)

Connect

We are designed to be social creatures — to unify ourselves with others. When we are unified, we are stronger, healthier, and better able to navigate the twists and turns of life. We cannot truly thrive in isolation. Believe me — I tried. Oh, if you knew of me during my difficult times, you would have thought that I was Miss Congeniality. But I didn't truly let anyone in — only Madison, and I obviously couldn't share everything with her. I loved others fully, and I saw them, embraced them, celebrated them, cherished them. I had precious friends whom I adored. I just didn't let them fully see me, embrace me, or know me; I hid my reality in embarrassment and shame. I turned down invitations to go places; I feigned that I was busy when I really craved deeper connections. My self-imposed isolation weakened my spirit and my sense of self, transforming me into a shell of who I was born to be.

I had never felt more alone than I did during those difficult years of my life. Yet, I still didn't tell anyone. Until Mona.

Mona Hurley is truly one of the most magnificent women on this planet. She exemplifies grace, wisdom, and understanding. She exudes love to everyone, and I have never met anyone who did not simply adore her. I had the privilege of teaching in the classroom next to hers when my life fell apart. Although I didn't open up to her at first, I would often find myself craving just to be near her; her peaceful, loving spirit somehow kept my inner turmoil at bay. Whenever she gave me one of her famous hugs, it provided me with the comfort I needed to keep moving forward.

One day after school, Mona came into my classroom. "Kim, you are doing a great job."

"Thank you, Mona," I replied, thinking she was referencing my lesson.

She gently continued, "You are doing a great job at fooling everyone, but you are not fooling me. What is it, sweetie? When you smile, your eyes are so sad."

In that moment, my walls started to crack. I so desperately needed someone to talk to, someone to trust, someone to hold me and tell me it would be okay. So, I poured it all out. Once I began, I could not stop. I told her of my pain, my sorrow, my truth. Mona did everything you would want someone to do. She listened, she cried with me, she held me, she prayed with me. She stayed with me for as long as I needed.

That night when I went home, I slept through the night for the first time since the whole ordeal had begun. I felt supported; I felt stronger. *I can do this*, I thought. In the months that followed, Mona was always there to check on me with a listening ear, hugs, and words of comfort and strength. She never judged, she never pushed, she never told me what to do. She just supported me in my time of greatest need.

The day after I found that cell phone in the back seat of the car, I asked Mona if I could go to her house. She held me for what must have been hours as my shattered being sobbed. She gave me strength, she gave me hope, she gave me unconditional love, and for the rest of my life, no words of appreciation will ever be enough. She is the woman I strive to be; she is the epitome of all that is good in this world. My wish for you, my friend, is that you find a Mona. My wish is also that you *be* a Mona — a bright light that shines love, mercy, grace, kindness, and goodness onto others.

When I came to the point in my life when I realized I could not do things alone, everything changed. Needing and accepting help did not make me weak; it made me human. I decided that from then on, I would surround myself with people who fuel my soul — the Monas of this world. I would trust myself to trust them . . . to break down my walls and build bridges.

Needing and accepting help did not make me weak; it made me human.

Do you erect walls, too? If you have been hurt, it is easy to put up barriers for self-preservation, but we are created to love and be loved. I am not talking about finding a spouse here. I am talking about our day-to-day interactions in this world — ones where we feel positively connected to others. You might be quiet, you might be shy, but there are quiet, shy people who have beautiful, meaningful friendships. You don't have to have hundreds of friends, just a small circle who knows you fully for who you are, a circle whom you can trust and count on for help. You might have been hurt, but there are good people out there who will not hurt you. Perhaps you have numerous acquaintances; perhaps you have tens of thousands of followers on social media; perhaps you are surrounded by hundreds of people at your job each day — yet, you might not have any friends who truly *know* you. Do you change who you are to project an image, or do you have a circle with whom you are able to be your authentic self?

How do you find meaningful relationships? Look for the people who are serving, uplifting, and doing good. They are the types of friends you want to have. Avoid the gossipers, the rude, the naysayers, and the selfish. Stay away from the unkind, the angry, the jealous, and the cruel. Be polite to them, but look to those who nurture your soul when seeking true friendships. We are designed with a purpose, and that purpose involves doing something in this world that will in some way benefit humankind; find those who are living life in such a way. You might have to put yourself out there to make this happen; you might have to join a club or find a place to volunteer. And while you are building these relationships, remember to nurture some meaningful relationships with those who do not look just like you.

Love

After a long day at work, I was forced to visit my least favorite place on Earth: the grocery store. As we pulled into the crowded parking lot, I sighed. Phakamani and Sabelo had far more energy than I, so they volunteered to go inside to get our needed items.

As we sat in the car, thirteen-year-old Sisipho, ever joyful, cranked the radio up full blast and started to sing to me with great fanfare. I couldn't help but laugh, and my mood significantly lightened. As he sang, he started to poke me in the ribs and tickle me. The more I giggled, the more he poked. I squealed and giggled as I fought with him and tried to grab him, but he was too fast. As I tried to twist his hand, he wriggled free and sang even louder.

And then I saw her. A middle-aged white woman sat in the car beside us, her face stricken with panic. She stared at me wide-eyed, grabbed her cell phone, and frantically turned it on.

And then I panicked, too. "Sisipho, stop!" I said, my voice changing.

He laughed and continued.

Fumbling, the woman started punching numbers while still staring intently.

"Sisipho! STOP! I mean it!" I whisper-yelled into his ear while trying to keep smiling. And then, "Quick—hug me. Now!"

Baffled, he leaned in to hug me, and I caught the sadness in his eyes. I had startled him, confused him, and hurt him.

I held him tightly, smiled wanly, and glanced back at the woman as she put her phone down. I waved at her as she put her car in drive and pulled away.

"I am sorry, Ma. Did I hurt you?" Sisipho asked.

"No, baby. You didn't hurt me, but that woman . . . well . . . she thought you were hurting me."

"Oh." He put his head down. And my heart shattered.

Would that woman have thought the same thing if I had been with a thirteen-year-old white boy? I don't know for sure, but somehow, I doubt it. I was laughing, yet her eyes expressed terror. Yes, she was a concerned citizen who thought I was being hurt, and she appeared to be trying to help. But what caused such profound fear? Was it that I was a white woman in a car being tickled by a boy, or was it because he was a strong black boy? That woman might have had the best of intentions, but I assume that her concern was caused by her own fears—fears that many share but will not admit.

The younger version of me could never have imagined that one day I would be the mother to three beautiful, black African boys. I never could have imagined that I would be horrified and heartbroken that someone could fear my precious, kind, loving sons. This reality is especially hard for me to swallow and comprehend. My boys grow taller, stronger, and more handsome each day. And yet, I know that with this transition to manhood comes this truth: they now have the power to frighten and intimidate some people, even without trying. Their mere presence can be seen as a threat, simply because of deep-seated fears that stem from ignorance.

So, I now experience new fears of my own—namely, the fear that when my boys leave my home, they will not be seen for the goodness they possess, but rather as the compilation of traits that have been rooted in minds from the spread of hatred, inaccuracies, and ignorance. I am terrified that they will be seen as living manifestations of ungrounded racist beliefs instead of the fine young men that they are. How do I protect them from a portion of society that will judge them based solely on the color of their skin?

My boys joined our family at age twelve, and when it was time for their first Halloween in America, they were ecstatic. Their costumes were a little eccentric. They were intrigued by the multiple options at the costume store, so I found myself surrendering to the idea of a vampire ninja, a zombie, and a warrior. Basically, each was adorned from head to toe in black and was embellished with all the cool scars, wounds, and tattoos one could ever hope for. Their friend Jacob invited them to join him and their classmates on his street, a long road in a highly urban area of Atlanta that was known to be a trick-or-treaters' paradise. Since we lived right around the corner, I thought it sounded like a great idea.

Not long after their departure, someone posted on our neighborhood Facebook page to "be on the lookout." Apparently three teenagers, dressed in all black, were breaking into cars. The neighbors were rightfully concerned and shared their thoughts on a string of posts. I, however, couldn't breathe. What if someone thought my twelve-year-old boys were the ones who were committing the crimes? What if someone hurt them? I hadn't told them how to respond if someone confronted them. I had only loved them and encouraged them. But I had never had *the talk*.

If you don't know about *the talk*, it is because you have never needed to.

Growing up, I never thought about what it was to be white. I just was. But through my interactions with my friends of color, I now understand that black children must be taught what it is to be black. How they navigate this world, how they respond to others, whom they trust, how they live, shop, drive . . . there is a caution that stems from their reality that requires lessons on how to be black in our world. You don't have to believe me, but it is so. I experienced the fear of what it means to be the mother of black boys for the first time on that Halloween night, and now, battling this fear for their safety is a part of my reality.

Fear is a complex, limiting thing. Fear of abandonment leads us to cling too tightly or to build barriers to avoid relationships. Fear of failure often paralyzes us or creates workaholics. Fear of being upstaged creates jealousy or the need to put down others. Fear of success leads to self-sabotage. Sometimes our fears are completely justified; there are evil people in this world who commit evil deeds. But far too often, we have unjustifiable fears, simply because we do not understand. When we fear, we imagine the worst-case scenario and obsess over it. We allow our minds to go to dark places where pain, hurt, and terror abound.

I long for a world where we don't fear other people without reason and where we acknowledge our fears and seek to understand them. Yes, there are bad people who do horrific things, and we must use discernment. But I pray for a world where we interact with others who are different than we are; I pray for unity. I have learned to be intentional about creating close friendships with, having meaningful conversations with, and getting to know those who have walked a different path, and I will never stop seeking to understand. When we look at others whom we do not understand, we sometimes think of them as representations of all of our preconceived ideas, notions, biases, and stereotypes. And we all have them — every single one of us, even if you do not want to admit that it is so. Fear and ignorance create messages — both direct and subtle — that can perpetuate pain for others that can fester for a lifetime. Once I developed and deepened relationships with others who are different than me, my worldview expanded. My love cast out misconceptions and taught me to see people — *truly* see people — as I believe my God would want me to see them.

I implore you to develop friendships with those who are not just like you. Seek out relationships — not just acquaintances, not just pleasantries. And I am not just talking about black and white. I am talking about every kind of diversity. Seek meaningful relationships with those who have walked a different path and have seen the world through a different lens — those who live, love, look, and worship differently than you do. I promise you that both your world and your worldview will be enriched.

Now you might be thinking, *Well, Kim, everyone within a twenty-five-mile radius kind of looks like me and worships like me!* I am certainly not implying that this makes you a bad person or a bigot. However, if this is the case, I do ask you to consider reading books that might not have ever interested you before and watching films that you never would have watched. Do so with an open mind. Do all you can to learn because, in the process, your heart will grow immeasurably. Your capacity to love will multiply.

To be clear, I continuously use the word *seek* because, quite honestly, we can never fully understand what it is to walk in another's shoes. For example, even though I have three black sons, I still navigate the world as a blonde

High school freshmen
(photo by Melissa White)

white woman. How I am treated and live life is, in part, affected by this white-ness. And quite honestly, for most of my life, I didn't even realize it. I am not saying there is anything wrong with being a white woman. I am saying, how-ever, that my life's experiences are impacted by it.

When my boys were freshmen in high school, we went to a public library to get their first library cards. I explained the whole process to them on the way there — I told them it should just take a few minutes to get the paperwork done and that I wanted them to take the lead. (I am big on nurturing inde-pendence in my children.) Upon entering the library, my sons approached the checkout desk. Sabelo politely looked at the librarian and said, "Hello, ma'am. The three of us would like to get library cards."

She looked the three of them up and down and said, "Okay. I need just a few moments." She clicked away on her computer, and eventually looked up and said she would be right back. She returned with the forms and handed them to them. She started to go over the guidelines for using the library — she reiterated that it was a place that should be quiet so that others would be able to work. I felt like this was obvious, and her emphasis on this raised my mama antennae ever so slightly. My boys politely nodded, listened, and occasionally interjected with "Yes, ma'am."

She noted that since the boys were under eighteen, they would need a parent signature on the forms. And then she said, "Are you boys sure you *really* want library cards? You can just use the materials here in the library. If you check out materials and do not return them, you will have to pay for them."

Oh. No. She. Didn't.

Look, my previous book was all about how to effectively communicate with others, to uplift them, to come together. But there was also a chapter in that book about confrontation, and this was definitely a time for it.

I stepped forward. "Ma'am, isn't the point of a library for people — especially students — to have a place to check out books? Isn't that why you are here?"

"Ye . . . yes," she stammered.

"Then my sons would like to get their library cards. My sons will return any materials that they check out. Is there a reason you would assume they would not?" I felt Sabelo start to tug at my elbow. He sensed my blood boiling, even though I continued to be polite.

"These are your sons?" she asked.

"Yes. And we would like the library cards please. My sons are dedicated students, and they are excited about the opportunity to have access to the materials here. You mentioned that they would need a parent signature. Where do I need to sign?"

She responded, "I am going to need some type of proof that they are your sons."

What the heck?

I responded, "Ma'am, what kind of proof are you asking for?"

"Proof that you are their mother," she said.

"Ma'am, am I to understand that every time a parent comes in here with a child to get a library card, you ask for proof that they are indeed the parent? There was nothing on your website that said this would be necessary."

"Well, um, no . . . but they do not look like you," she added.

"Ma'am, my sons are obviously adopted. So, do all parents of adopted children have to provide some kind of additional proof of adoption in order to get a library card?" I asked.

She responded, "Well, no, but . . ."

Phakamani interrupted, "It's okay, Mom. Let's just go."

I continued, "Ma'am, can I speak to your supervisor, just to be clear on your policies? It seems that you are providing information that is different from what is on your website, and I want to make sure you are not adding requirements that are specifically geared toward my sons."

Just as I was saying this, as if on cue, the head librarian walked out of the back office.

"How can I help you?" she warmly asked. I calmly relayed the discussion and explained that we had been asked to provide proof that I was my sons' mother. She seemed truly stunned. She looked at the other librarian and said, "I have this now. Can you go into my office and wait for me?"

The head librarian was sincere, gracious, and apologetic. She gave my boys a tour of the library, and she asked them all about school, their hobbies, and their interests. She was lovely. As we prepared to depart, she stopped and said, "I am so very sorry that you all were treated like you are not welcome here. You have my word that I will handle the situation. If ever you boys come back to this branch, you will always be treated with respect."

My sons all gave her a hug as we left. Their capacity to love and forgive filled my heart.

Privilege

That day in the library may seem like an isolated incident, but I could write a whole book with nothing but stories such as this — situations that have happened with my sons, my students, my coworkers, and my friends. I lived most of my life without ever even knowing the constant microaggressions that many face on a daily basis, and now that I do know, I must call them out for what they are. You might be reading this and think, *Well, what is the big deal?* But imagine if, day in and day out, even things as simple as getting a library card were more challenging for you. It would wear you down, break your heart, and possibly even break your spirit.

Earlier I shared with you how I talked myself onto that airplane without an ID. And later I'll tell you about the time I walked into a kitchen in a Japanese hotel where we were staying long after it was closed. That simple action terrified my coworkers. In my mind, I was paying to stay in the hotel; therefore, the kitchen should be accessible to me . . . to us.

Another example: A couple of years ago, there was a new neighborhood being built near my neighborhood, and while out jogging, I wanted to take a look inside the houses to see what they looked like. I walked into the garage of one and found the door unlocked and entered to scope it out without so much as a blink of an eye. I came home and casually mentioned it to my sons, and their friends who were visiting freaked out. "Mrs. Bearden, you can't just go walking into houses like that!"`

"Why not? They will be for sale soon. I was just looking around!"

"Never mind," they said, realizing the difference. Now I do, too. Privilege.

I stay in many hotels when I give speeches. My routine is the same: on the way out, I will pop into the small store beside the checkout desk to grab a drink and something small for breakfast. I usually say, "Can you please add this to room 209?" and walk out. I never show my key or an ID. After traveling with my friends of color, I know they always have to show a room key and ID. Privilege.

When it was my sons' first Christmas here, I went to the store to find some black Santa Clauses to add to my collection. I went to an area of town where the population was predominately black, yet I could only find one black Santa among dozens of others. In Soweto, South Africa, I shopped for baby dolls for the children in the orphanage, yet I could only find white ones. Most characters in books look like me; most actors on screen do, too. Even "flesh"-colored Band-Aids match my skin. I remember the hallway of my childhood church — it was lined with paintings of my Jesus, but he was a blonde-haired, blue-eyed version instead of the olive-skinned, Palestinian Jewish man that He truly was. The disciples looked more like me, too. I have never had to look for representation or validation, and I should never take this for granted.

One day, I was running late to work, and admittedly, I ran through a red light. (Well, I thought it was more of a yellowish-orange.) I turned left, drove one mile, turned right, entered through the gates of RCA, whipped into a parking space, jumped out of my car, and ran smack-dab into a police man.

Startled, I said, "Excuse me, officer! I apologize! Is everything okay?" I hoped nothing was happening at the school.

"Ma'am, we have been following you with our lights on since you ran that red light," he said.

Eek. "Um, I apologize, officer. I was running late, and there is no excuse."

"So, you work here?" he asked.

"Yes, sir."

"Please slow down, ma'am. Thank you for being a teacher."

He was so kind, and I was grateful. There are amazing, hardworking police officers who risk their lives for us all every day, and I let him know that I appreciated his service. Then he left.

However, three weeks later, one of our staff members accidentally ran that same red light on a left-hand turn. Different police officers put on their lights, and our staff member pulled over immediately. The two officers approached the vehicle . . . with guns drawn. Our staff member, a black man, stared at the barrel of a gun held to his window, trembling. Hands on the wheel. He was still. He did exactly as he was asked as he received a ticket. When he walked into the school, he was visibly shaken — so much so, that I tried to send him home, but he would not go.

"Mrs. Bearden, this is my reality." Then, he cried.

He was a professional black male, a teacher, dressed in a suit and tie. A yellow light turned red while he was turning, he immediately pulled over, and he had to stare down the barrel of a gun. See the difference?

Yes, I have experienced tremendous pain and heartache — some of which I poured into this book. I have shared my sorrows with you, but even when I was $212,000 in debt, I never feared being homeless. My family was never considered wealthy by American standards, but my great-grandparents owned modest homes, and then so did my grandparents and my parents. Their homes were small and simple; however, they still owned them. Each generation worked hard to leave something to their children, which is beautiful. But what if my great-grandparents and grandparents were denied such opportunities, even though they worked hard, too? What if each future generation had to work to support the previous one instead of vice versa?

What if I had to take care of my parents financially to ensure that they had food on the table? This may be you, or it may be a foreign concept to you. If you have never struggled to pay bills, you cannot imagine how poverty wears down the soul; if you have not sought out friendships with those who have struggled, you cannot even begin to comprehend. You might even think, "Well, they should just work harder." Some of the hardest-working people I know have multiple college degrees and good jobs, yet they are crippled by student loans, and their salaries are used to take care of family members who did not have such opportunities.

My journey toward understanding continues to unfold, with all its beauty and complexity. The more I learn, the more I realize I do not know. I make mistakes, I misstep, I misspeak. But I am bound and determined to work to create safe spaces where the conversation can take place and where unity is embraced and encouraged.

So, what does all of this have to do with taking back my life and finding purpose? Well, when I reflect upon my life's experiences and the factors that had the greatest impact upon who I am and how I see the world, expanding my circle to love *all* people has been the most helpful, healing, good, and true thing I have ever done. Seeking unity and experiencing that type of love for humankind makes us, well, more human and kind.

As a young girl, I played the clarinet. I was quite good, and I would practice diligently every day. However, I never really enjoyed playing alone.

> Seeking unity and experiencing
> that type of love for humankind makes us,
> well, more human and kind.

Performing solo never matched the euphoric feeling of sitting in the middle of the symphonic band, engulfed by the trilling woodwinds, bellowing brass, and pounding drums. The mellifluous sounds — all different — would float over me, above me, through me, and into my soul. It was the mingling, mixed melodies, cadences, chords, tones, tempos, vibrations, and vibratos that made it all so exciting and beautiful. Sure, I could play a lovely tune on my own, but if you put me with completely different and varied instruments, then the magic truly began to unfold. I feel like our lives are the same way. Who wants to go through life only surrounded by other clarinets?

When you are able to see beyond yourself, beyond your inner circle, you start to understand that the universe is vast and wide; it does not revolve around you. There is sorrow everywhere, but there is also love to be found. It is our job to seek it, nurture it, and protect it. It is our job to realize the glory of living in a world where we are each created to be unique, magnificent, and embraced for who we were born to be.

Care

When we have meaningful relationships, our lives are enriched; connections are the harmony to our melody. Relationships create the depth and breadth of our purpose; they give us hope and healing. It has been found that meaningful relationships can even increase our lifespan. Trauma can have a lifelong impact upon our ability to function — it can affect our emotional, intellectual, and physical well-being, even into adulthood; adversity can affect the biology of our brains and impact our health. However, it is believed that forging bonds with others is one of the most impactful ways for someone to heal and lead a fulfilling life.

I wanted to share this concept with my staff; I wanted them to know that when they build relationships with our students, they are helping students heal for a lifetime. My staff is phenomenal about lifting up others and supporting our children and one another, and I hoped for them to fully recognize their impact upon others. To illustrate my point, I bought several boxes of Kerplunk, a game where a cylindrical tube is filled with sticks that support marbles. As each player removes a stick, the goal is that no marbles fall to the bottom. I then made a deck of sixty cards, with each card containing a situation that causes pain or trauma, such as:

- Your parents are divorcing.
- You are hungry.
- Your father is imprisoned.
- You have a chronic illness.
- You are homeless.
- You are verbally abused.

Mixed in with these cards, I added "support" cards about positive relationships, such as:

- Your mentor met with you.
- You eat lunch every day with an adult and some of your friends.
- Your teacher tutored you.
- You shared your frustrations, and someone listened and helped.
- You feel like your teacher supports you.

I then told my staff that the Kerplunk cylinder represented a child. The marbles represented the child's brain and his/her ability to learn, and the sticks represented stressors. I then gave each group pipe cleaners, and I told them that these represented positive relationships. To play the game, each person drew a card. If it contained a stressor, a stick was removed, often resulting in marbles falling to the bottom. However, whenever a positive card was drawn, my staff was able to add pipe cleaners, strengthening the child's ability to hold onto the marbles (thoughts, knowledge, and ideas). There was no winner of the game; it was really more of a simulation. The takeaway? The more supportive relationships we have, the better we are able to function. Without the support, we become broken and defeated; we lose our great potential to thrive. It was a powerful reminder of the importance of positive interactions and rapport.

People often ask Ron and me for the secrets to our school's success. Well, for one thing, we work hard. Our hearts are fully committed to helping children. But probably the biggest secret is really no secret at all: it is the people we hire. The people with whom we surround ourselves. People like our facilities manager, Mr. Johnny Mills.

As the sixth-grade girls stumbled around an ice-skating rink for the first time in their lives, I watched in complete amusement. They reminded me of newborn baby fawns — their spindling legs could not hold them up, and the more they tried to balance themselves, the more they toppled over, continuously pulling one another onto the ice in a heap of giggles, mittens, and braids.

They weren't the only ones giggling. Behind me, I turned to see Johnny, shoulders bouncing with his trademark laughter. I looked down to see that he, too, was wearing skates for the first time.

"Are you going to go help them, Johnny?" I teased.

"I am having a hard time even walking to the edge of the ice, but I am working on it!" he replied.

For the next hour, Johnny tumbled and crashed into everyone and everything on the ice. The girls, who still could not skate well themselves, grabbed his arms, and they all devised a method of stopping that involved ramming into the sides of the rink, shaking them with pounding thunder. Each time Johnny would let go of the girls, he would forget the whole concept of skating and would instead try to run on the ice. His feet would fly up in the air, and he would land on his behind with a massive thud. I was certain he was going to break something, but he was relentless. The girls were overjoyed, and I can still see Ciara doubled over with laughter, the pink pompom on her hat bobbing, even though ten years have passed.

Johnny made us all laugh, but he also always supported us. He would bring treats to my room — just because — and smile broadly; he would check on everyone just to make sure we didn't need anything. Johnny had worked hard his whole life, yet he always did it with such joy, such dedication, and loyalty. He loved our kids, our staff, our parents . . . and we loved him.

When Johnny started to have aches in his leg, he attributed it to his age. He would continue to push through the pain, even when I would implore him to stop and sit down. Sometimes, I would see him wince, but he would turn to me and make a joke about being old, and those shoulders would bounce up and down again.

Johnny loved the Ron Clark Academy, and he took great pride in looking out for us all. I had to fuss at him for sneaking to work on weekends without logging his hours. He said he just needed to "check on a few things," which meant that he wanted to make sure that everything in the school shone and that the aroma of Fabulosa wafted throughout the halls when everyone entered on Monday.

But the pain continued, and finally, stubborn, wonderful Johnny went to the doctor. It was cancer. It did not stop him, though. Every day, Johnny would remain at work, surrounded by those who loved him. One day I found him sitting in a chair in my room, massaging his leg.

"Johnny — go home!"

"Mrs. Bearden, during the day I am the happiest when I am here, surrounded by my RCA family. Once my wife, Denise, gets off of work, I will head home to be with her."

So, Johnny would come to work, even after the chemo began. Some days, he would insist on helping out. Most days, he just wanted to be with everyone. Our staff pitched in to help with some of Johnny's duties — that is what family does. We thought he had beaten it all and was on the road to recovery, but eventually, it came back and spread throughout his body.

When he was finally bedridden at home, our staff rotated our visits so someone from his RCA family could always be by his side whenever his wife and grown children could not. The men of RCA made sure his yard was in order — something that Johnny always took pride in doing.

I had always been fascinated by Johnny's hands. Weather-beaten, calloused, and rough, they told a story of a man who had labored hard. When I visited Johnny for the last time, I held his leathery palm in mine, and we laughed about the day-to-day happenings at RCA. We recounted stories, and Johnny had to know how every single person in the building was doing. He wasn't just being polite — he genuinely cared. Throughout our lives, people are placed in our paths to teach us how to be better than we were before encountering them, and Johnny was one of those people. He was our hero until the end — even after the end, for his laughter still lives in our hallways.

Throughout our lives, people are placed in our paths to teach us how to be better than we were before encountering them.

Johnny Mills with Sabelo
(photo by J. Amezqua)

Engage

Losing both Johnny and Ryan was unbearable, and the hearts of our staff and students broke. Sometimes when we feel such loss, we get lost inside of ourselves; we retreat because there simply are no words. It aches to talk about the grief that ebbs and flows in waves of sorrow. But I knew that together we would be better; I knew that Johnny would have wanted that. I needed to bring our staff together so we could be stronger for our students and one another, so I devised a plan for our teacher workday.

I bought some inexpensive, small, square tiles, hammers, grout, and a huge piece of wood. I spray-painted the tiles with beautiful colors, and I set up everything in my classroom. I placed the wood in the center with the tiles, hammers, and some towels around it. As the staff entered, I asked them to sit on the floor in a circle amid the materials.

I picked up some of the tiles and placed them under my towel. I raised my hammer and said, "Ryan passed away." As I said it, I smashed the tile with all my might. We could hear it shatter beneath the towel.

"Johnny passed away." Smash.

"My mother passed away with Alzheimer's." Smash.

"My father's Parkinson's is getting worse." Smash.

I signaled for others to pick up tiles and hammers and to smash away at every bit of rage, every bit of pain, every bit of sorrow they were feeling in their own lives. It was a release; in the words of my daughter, it was the storm before the rainbow.

Once we had stopped, I shared. "We have all experienced individual pain, but we will not be defeated. We will live and love even harder to keep Johnny's and Ryan's legacies alive. We are broken, but together we are beautiful."

I then instructed everyone to pick up their pieces, and together, we created a mosaic out of all of the shattered tiles. As we wove our colorful fragments together upon the board, a beautiful piece of art emerged. We stood around it and joined hands as we finished. Tears streamed down our faces, but they were tears of gratitude for the love we had shared and the memories that no one could ever take away. We hugged each other; we spoke into one another. We had been broken, but we were unified. Stronger. We knew each other better. Together, we were better.

In my most difficult hours, I always felt unbearable loneliness, but I know that it was I who had isolated myself. I had loyal, dedicated friends and family who would do anything for me, yet I had retreated into my own private hell. Oh, I smiled, laughed, and put on a brave face, but I was hiding my sadness. I was a phenomenal actress. Well, at least I thought I was.

I want better for you, my friend. I am not telling you to go on social media and tell the whole world your business; you don't have to pour it out in a book. But you must engage, not retreat. You must share, not suppress. You must release. Shatter tiles with a hammer; punch your pillow; run as far as your legs can take you; cry until you have no tears left. But there is peace after the storm, and I want you to embrace it with others. When we share our joy, it is magnified tenfold. And when we all share the burdens of our challenges, they are no longer so heavy to bear.

When we share our joy, it is magnified tenfold. And when we all share the burdens of our challenges, they are no longer so heavy to bear.

Notes

♪ We should surround ourselves with people who fuel our souls.

♪ We are designed to be social creatures who unify ourselves with others.

♪ Needing and accepting help does not make us weak; it makes us human.

♪ Build bridges that develop meaningful relationships.

♪ Look for friends who are noble, kind, honorable, and true.

♪ Seek out relationships with those who have walked a different path; seek to understand.

♪ Acknowledge implicit bias and strive to love all people.

♪ Connections with others can help us overcome adversity and trauma.

♪ When we are broken, our unity can strengthen us and make us better.

Change Your Tune

♪ Reflect upon the meaningful relationships in your life. How can you continue to make time to nurture them?

♪ Identify any relationship barriers (walls) that you have created for yourself. How can you make them into bridges?

♪ Seek out relationships with people who exhibit traits that you would like to see in yourself.

♪ Seek out relationships with people who do not look like you. Make meaningful connections. In the very least, make it a goal to read books and watch documentaries or movies about people who are different than you. Watch with an open heart and mind.

♪ Recognize and take actions against the fact that social media feeds us information that confirms our perceived points of view. Search out other ideas, delve into history, or research to make sure you know and articulate truth, not bias.

♪ Engage with others in your times of darkness; do not retreat.

chapter **5**

Identify

Modify

Amplify

Unify

(**Fortify**)

Battle Cry

When we FORTIFY ourselves,
we strengthen ourselves so we can better
fulfill our life's purpose and passion.

2011 I inhale the crisp spring air as I stretch and flex my muscles, preparing for the course. I've been in training for months, for I am a Spartan. Well, at least that's what my registration form says. The Spartan Race is both a race and an obstacle course unlike anything I have ever done in my life. I want to push myself to be stronger, and so do Ron, Junior, and our alumni—Jai, Jordan, and Osei—who join us for the big event.

When the starting whistle blows, I dart down the trail into the woods, adrenaline rushing through me. I scale ten-foot walls, climb ropes, and wade through streams. I carry a sack of cement up a mountain, shoot spears at targets, pull myself up massive slickened ramps, and flip tractor tires with chains. Perhaps the most exhilarating part, though, is crawling the length of a football field filled with gooey mud, laboriously inching forward on my stomach beneath barbed wire. The mud is so thick that it seeps into my clothing, making it even harder to progress. If I lift too high off the ground, I will be cut by the razor-sharp barbs, so I continue to shimmy and slink through the ooze. I am so tickled by it all that I cannot stop giggling. All around me, others slop along as well, and I find it completely absurd that we would subject ourselves to this. In fact, we have actually paid to do it.

Weary and determined, I finally head for the finish line, only to encounter muscled men in Spartan attire whose job is to thwart my success. They hold huge cushioned mallets, and as I pass each, I have to dip and dive to avoid being knocked to the ground. The finish line grows ever closer, but I feel like I'm not quite ready for this experience to end. Then I see it — one of the giant mallets left lying on a bale of hay that lines the course. I grab it, turn away from the finish line, and run back into the gauntlet. I dash toward the biggest Spartan, swing my mallet, and hit him on his back with all of my might. He whips around, utterly shocked, and proceeds to chase me as the other Spartans follow suit. Ducking, bobbing, weaving, I dodge the Spartans as they chase me across the finish line. I finish the race in grand style, laughing the whole way.

When they place my Spartan medal around my neck, I feel an enormous wave of satisfaction, pride, and appreciation. At forty-six years of age, I have pushed myself, tried my hardest, and encountered every obstacle with a sense of resolve. I am no longer the weak girl who lies on my closet floor in tears. Finishing the race means something because I have worked so diligently and overcome so much to get here — it makes it all so much sweeter.

For days, I proudly display my cuts and bruises — the battle scars of my success. Later, I share my medal with my students. I am officially a Spartan, a strong physical beast at the pinnacle of good health.

The Spartan Race

ne month after the Spartan Race, I quit working out and gained ten pounds. I forgot that life is a marathon, not an isolated race. This is not a chapter about losing weight, I promise. If you want a book about that, you will find it somewhere else. I think we need to be healthy, but healthy and beautiful come in all shapes and sizes . . . despite the fact that we see images and receive messages to the contrary every day. However, this is a chapter about growing stronger in body, mind, and spirit.

Move

When we fortify ourselves, we strengthen ourselves so we can better fulfill our life's purpose and passion. Sometimes we are so busy taking care of everyone else that we forget that we have to strengthen ourselves to be strong for others. This is a lesson I am still learning. But as I grow older, I certainly view the gift of our bodies differently — especially since things have changed with my dad.

Ten years ago, I received a phone call five minutes before my seventh-grade class entered the room. It was my daddy.

"Honey, I have some sad news to share with you. I have been diagnosed with Parkinson's disease," he said. "I am fine now, but things will progressively get worse."

I remember nothing else from that phone call, but I do remember that the class of 2011 walked into my room while I was still on the phone, tears streaming down my face. Stunned, they stood still with mixed expressions of concern and panic. I hung up, quickly wiping my tears away.

"I am okay, y'all. I just found out that my daddy is sick . . ." My voice cracked as the students immediately surrounded me with one massive group hug. They didn't know what to say, but no words were needed. Their display of love was perfect. They just held me until I was able to swallow the tears and get myself together. I drew strength from their outpouring of affection.

Parkinson's is a cruel neurological disease that affects people differently but ultimately leads to tremors, rigidity, and the loss of body movement. It is as if the body becomes stone, unable to bend or turn; it slowly shuts down, making even the simplest of tasks impossible. My father has been a valiant warrior as he has fought to stay mobile and active. In fact, we had to hide the car keys a couple of years ago because he was so stubborn. But now in the final stages, Daddy cannot use his legs, he cannot use his arms, and only one hand works. He cannot feed himself, relieve himself, or bathe himself. It takes two people to lift him from the bed to his electric wheelchair, and his only working hand now struggles to steer it. Parkinson's also often leads to delusions and hallucinations, but thus far, my father has been spared those horrific symptoms. My big brother Bobby lives close to my father and visits him every single day. He is an amazing son.

I live a little over an hour away, so for me, Saturdays are Daddy Days. I feed Daddy lunch and talk to him about my week. I comb his hair because he finds it relaxing—he never feels truly comfortable because his body is rigid and cannot move. I place a small ball in the palm of his hand to open it enough to be able to give him a manicure. I massage his arms with lotion. I hug him because he longs for physical affection but cannot hug back. He cannot hear well or see well, so I must holler to communicate with him, but I try nonetheless. I give thanks for the life he led, but I push back tears at the life he now leads. He is ready to go be with God and my mother. He often tells me this. It is not morbid—he does not fear death, nor should he. He wants to be free from pain, and I understand. Perhaps he will have passed by the time you read these words. Perhaps I will still be with him as you read this, cherishing the opportunity for another day to stroke his wavy hair and tell him that I love him.

Watching my father's fight has let me know just how much I take for granted. If you are able to walk, then please don't complain about walking far. Run, dance, twirl, skip. Bend, twist, lift. Reach, stretch, leap, and hug. Use the body you have been given and realize that it is a gift. Have you ever stopped to think about how many things your hands can do? Your feet? Your arms make it possible for you to embrace others, providing comfort, affection, and love. Your ears allow you experience the thunder of laughter and music; your

Daddy when he
was still healthy

eyes enable you to behold the glory of the sunset and the stars. Your tongue allows you to savor flavors and speak words into others; your heartbeat is the rhythm of your very being.

Since my father lost all movement in his body, I have started to do everything I can to keep mine moving. But Lord knows, it is so hard to find the time. I finally figured out something that works for me — I joined a fitness boot camp gym near my house, and I go to class at five thirty in the morning every day. To ensure that I follow through, I actually sleep in my workout clothes so that I can roll out of bed at the last possible moment and get there on time. To be honest, for years I obsessed about being thin; I grew up in an era where we were taught that we could never be skinny or tan enough. (I was that girl who lay out in the driveway slathered in baby oil. And yes, I have had several skin cancers removed as a result.) Finally, I have stopped worrying so much about my weight. I just want to be healthy and strong. I am so grateful for the powerful, strong, curvy women who are now redefining beauty and health to be something more attainable. My fifty-four-year-old body doesn't look the same as it once did, but I have regained my Spartan strength and can flip tires and do a crazy number of sit-ups, push-ups, burpees, and planks. I am going to keep moving and giving thanks as long as I can. It is possible that I, too, will have Parkinson's one day, but I will do my darndest to fight until the end, just like my beloved daddy.

Not only have I watched my father suffer; my precious mama died of Alzheimer's disease several years ago. I wrote the story of her passing in my previous book, so I will not share it here. It would just be too much sorrow all at once. However, I must share that she was a wonderful mother who exemplified unconditional love, and I am finally able to focus on the memories of who she *was* before she *wasn't*; I am able to replay only the best of times when I reminisce. There is not a day that I do not miss her. Lately, she has visited me in my dreams. Watching her mind fade away was both heart-wrenching and terrifying. On more than one occasion, I have wondered if I will face the same fate. And what if I have Alzheimer's *and* Parkinson's?

There is no cure for either disease, but there is research about Alzheimer's that is helpful. Doctors stress that factors that lead to overall health can at least help prolong the onset, such as healthy sleep, eating, and exercise habits. It is important to keep the mind sharp — never stop learning, reading, and challenging yourself. Take up a new hobby, play an instrument, study a new language, build things, paint pictures. Just keep pushing your mind to do new things or at least to do old things better than before. Our minds are capable of extraordinary things; they can continue to grow throughout our lifetimes. My sons are a beautiful reminder of this.

> ## Our minds are capable of extraordinary things; they can continue to grow throughout our lifetimes.

Learn

My sons arrived here in the summer before their seventh-grade year. Scotty and I immediately began to work with them on academics, and we were both scared and overwhelmed when we realized the depth and breadth of their gaps in basic skills. As I mentioned before, they speak five languages, yet they were not literate in them. There are eleven official languages in South Africa, and my sons spoke Xhosa and Zulu in their homes. In school, they were taught to read and write in English, but their instruction was very limited. Sisipho could only read a few words, and I realized they were just words he recognized and had memorized. To write a sentence, he would say it into the phone and then laboriously type each letter that appeared on the screen. Sometimes, it would take five minutes for him to write just a phrase. I was so grateful for our staff—the amazing Kenneth Adams helped tutor my sons several times a week, and others poured into them before and after school. When we learned that Sisipho struggled to read, my friend Jennifer Salter, a phenomenal educator and tutor, regularly came to teach him phonics and reading skills. And still, Scotty and I needed to sit at the dining room table for several hours every night, rotating among the three boys. We didn't just need to help them with their current work; they had to learn all of the things they had never been taught. For the first year, I had to read them every page of every book aloud, stopping to put things into context for them. Sometimes, I feared it was all too much. Sometimes, I feared that Scotty and I would somehow fail them. Yet, with every day, every month, their minds grew faster and stronger. They started to find understanding; they grew more independent and more confident. My sons were brilliant. Determined. Driven. When they left the support that RCA provided and entered high school, we wondered how they would fare when starting over without teachers who had known them and grown so close to them and their story.

Not long after they began high school, I entered Sisipho's bedroom much earlier than usual one morning and found him reading a textbook.

"Hey, sweetie. I thought you finished your homework last night," I said.

"I did," he replied. "Since I still read more slowly than I would like, I get up every morning and pre-read anything that I think we might be doing in class. Plus, if I am asked to read aloud, I will already be familiar with the words since I have prepared myself," he answered.

My eyes pooled with tears as I threw my arms around him and held him tightly.

"What?" he laughed, hugging me back.

"Oh, my son, you are going to accomplish amazing things in this world."

As I write this, my sons are seniors in high school, and they do the work on their own. They make honor roll, they are leaders, they help others. We are currently in the midst of applying to colleges for all of them. If you were to visit my home, you might see Sabelo reading books on philosophy, studying history, or sketching a masterpiece. You might find Phakamani returning from his internship at a dentist office or working diligently on his soccer skills in the back yard.

And Sisipho? He never stops learning. Since arriving here, he has learned guitar, photography, movie making, music production, and acting. He is hired to take senior pictures, he makes videos for music groups, he does sound production for events, he directed his school play, and he deejays parties. He even interned on the set of *Queen Sugar*. He didn't take lessons for these things — he read and watched videos on YouTube.

I recently asked Sisipho what drives him. His answer? "When I was a kid in South Africa, I always believed I was born to do great things, even though I did not know how I would do them. I promised myself that I would take every opportunity I have to learn how to be better. I promised myself that if I learned how to read, I would read to learn. I promised myself that if I was ever fortunate to have a computer, I would use it to teach myself even more. I knew that I would use every opportunity I was given and be grateful for it." Oh, how I love my sons.

My Sisipho
(photo by J. Amezqua)

You, too, are born to do great things, my friend. Magnificent things. Things beyond your comprehension. You must believe this. Like Sisipho, you must promise yourself that you will take every opportunity to learn and grow, no matter how old you are.

When Ron and I started RCA, I was forty-one years old. I did not know how to create a nonprofit; I did not know how to raise funds from the community. I didn't know how to form a board of trustees or how to manage a building renovation. I didn't know how to write employment contracts. I had never built something from nothing. When I was told that we would need a business plan, I bought a copy of Business Plan Pro from Office Depot and taught myself how to write one. I knew how to be a teacher, an administrator, and a professional development trainer, but a school just like ours had never existed, so Ron and I had to figure most of it out on our own. We had to find people who could help us; we had to read books and articles and ask questions that would enable us to learn and grow. It was overwhelming, it was exhausting, and it was exhilarating. It was as if I could actually feel the dendrites in my head saying, "Heck, yeah, Kim! Let's keep growing and learning more!"

I know . . . sometimes we are so exhausted that we want to stare blankly at a television and zone out. That is fine and even necessary to do every once in a while. But please realize that we also energize and empower ourselves when we keep learning and growing. Read books. Peruse articles. Watch documentaries. Listen to podcasts and NPR. Fortify yourself with knowledge. It truly is a form of power. Realize that you have the power to determine what input you use to feed and occupy your mind.

Appreciate

It was the spring of my eighth-grade year, and I sat on my friend Linda's ruffled pink bedspread, tears streaming down my face. The source of my sadness was typical preteen angst—Linda's adorable neighbor liked someone else instead of me, and I was hurt when I discovered the truth. The situation seems absurd now, but at the time, the sting of it all was real. So, there I found myself, awash with preteen self-pity. After indulging me for several minutes, dear Linda hugged me tightly, and then said, "Wait!"

She darted out of the room and into the garage, where I heard her banging around. Consumed by my own drama, I just lay there wondering where on earth she had gone. A few minutes later, Linda's face shone as she ran into the bedroom. As she struggled to catch her breath, she said, "Follow me!" Linda grabbed my hand and led me out the back door and to a ladder she had placed against the house. Her kitchen windows had been propped open by large speakers, and music spilled into the yard. Up we climbed onto the roof and sat side by side.

From that vantage point, I could see an endless sea of identical ranch houses perfectly aligned in rows. Their symmetry somehow provided order amid the chaos in my young mind, and the tears started to dry. It was then that I looked higher to catch the gold, amber, and crimson colors painting the sunset sky, casting a glow upon the landscape. Linda said, "Wait. I want you to hear something." Smiling, she descended the ladder, entered the house, and quickly returned to my side. "Just listen."

The music, louder now, filled the air and encompassed me in a warm blanket as James Taylor's voice began to sing "Up on the Roof" to me. If you have never listened to the song, you must do so. The lyrics speak of the peace that can be found by simply sitting atop a roof and letting the cares of the world drift away.

Together, we sat arm in arm, and the tears tumbled onto my cheeks once again. However, this time, they were tears of gratitude. Appreciation rose up inside of me with such power, such intensity, that the moment is tattooed on my heart as one of my most vivid childhood memories. There we were — two innocent little girls with our whole lives ahead of us — and we sat arm in arm, peaceful, bonded, instinctively connected. Strength surged through me as I sat in awe and wonder, watching the sun descend. The warm Texas air filled my lungs, the music filled my soul, and our precious friendship filled my heart. It was the first time that I had ever sat still and just pondered the gift of beauty, of nature, of friendship, of life. Joy welled up within me and spilled out into laughter through the tears. I felt invincible.

When we occupy our minds and our time with positive influences, we affect our perspectives, our gratitude, and our ability to handle painful situations.

When we occupy our minds and our time with positive influences, we affect our perspectives, our gratitude, and our ability to handle painful situations.

We are fortified. My beloved childhood friend had wisely decided to occupy my thoughts with something other than self-pity; she helped me fill my mind with gratitude instead. It was a life lesson that remained with me and has sustained me at some of life's most challenging, painful moments. Our input definitely affects our output, much like making deposits at the bank. In order to have the power to uplift, serve, live, laugh, and love, we need to fill ourselves with beauty, kindness, goodness, and appreciation. Whatever fills our mind also fills our hearts and spills out of us and into the world. If we occupy ourselves with ugliness, hatred, anger, jealousy, insecurity, or selfishness, then we can become consumed by it. It can overtake us, leaving us weak and utterly broken.

Gratitude is one of life's most powerful forces. In fact, researchers have found that it can affect your mental well-being, stress levels, and even the ability to sleep better. When life is overwhelming us, we sometimes feel anything but grateful, but it is at those critical times that appreciation can have the greatest impact upon us. When we are hurting, we tend to be consumed by pain, and our internal lenses often focus on everything else that is wrong. If we choose to occupy our minds with the gratitude, however, it can diminish our sense of hopelessness. Gratitude changes perspective, and just as Linda showed me, it can be a wellspring of strength and hope.

For me, taking "gratitude walks" is a source of strength whenever I find myself overwhelmed or stressed. Here's how it works: I take a long walk, and the whole time, I focus on things for which I am grateful. I give thanks for things in nature, comforts I have been fortunate to have, people in my life, my work, my students, and my precious family. I give thanks for my ability to walk, to breath, to move. I methodically focus on even the smallest minutia, for sometimes it is the details that make a difference in our lives. I appreciate my heart beating, the wind in my hair, the sun on my back. I am thankful for the floating clouds, the falling leaves, and the flowers that bloom. After such a walk, I am always lighter, better, and happier. I learned this trick from my precious friend Chrissi Pepitone, RCA's extraordinary graphic designer who also just so happens to do Ironman challenges all the time. She is a beautiful, delicate, powerful, and fiercely competitive beast. Years ago, Chrissi sent me a text that simply said, "I want you to know that you are mile eight."

Confused, I gave her a call. "Mile eight?" I asked.

"Yes," she replied. "For the Ironman, we cannot listen to earphones or music, so every mile, I occupy my mind with thoughts of someone who is special to me. During mile eight, I will be thinking about memories, reflections, and experiences with you. It will motivate me along my journey."

I was so touched and so moved—it was the ultimate compliment. And it helped me to realize the power of ruminating on that which makes me grateful, happy, stronger, and better. It made me realize the necessity of surrounding myself with inspiration that fuels my soul. I need to let it wash over me, through me, and out into a world that is filled with trauma, pain, and obstacles beyond our control.

Relax

In case I haven't mentioned it enough, let me reiterate that I work with magnificent people—our staff is hardworking, determined, driven . . . and sometimes worn out. When you spend so much time uplifting others, you have to stop and refuel. You have to keep making deposits in order to have withdrawals. I always want to pour into them all, but I also recognize that we are all wired differently, and what soothes our souls varies from person to person. For you, running might bring you happiness; for another, that might seem like medieval torture. You might embrace classical music; another might feel like it is nails on a chalkboard. Keeping this in mind, I planned two very different activities for my staff to begin and end a recent workday.

As our team entered my darkened classroom that morning, yoga mats and towels covered the carpeted floor like a patchwork quilt. Candles glowed from around the room, and soothing spa music filled the space. At the front of the room sat Danielle, our instructor. She was surrounded by large glass bowls, gongs, rain sticks, and chimes. Her job was to give us all a sound bath, a multisensory experience where sounds and vibrations would wash over us, relaxing us. Okay, to be honest, I was a little nervous and skeptical when I booked the session, but I believe in the power of music and its ability to soothe, so I went for it.

As we lay upon the yoga mats on the floor, we closed our eyes and breathed deeply. Danielle artfully began to play her instruments, and the sounds coming from them can best be described as air, wind, rain, breath, and life. It was magnificent. Even more fascinating was the fact that we could feel the sounds — the vibrations caused binaural beats that washed over us. She spoke little — but she asked us to focus on good things that brought us happiness and peace; she asked us to meditate or pray about things for which we were thankful. When it was over, none of us wanted to leave — even those of us who had originally been skeptical. We were at peace, we were rejuvenated, we were strengthened, and we were able to hold hours of productive meetings afterward.

But remember — we are all different, so I provided our staff with a completely different experience after our work was finished. We loaded into the vans and drove to an undisclosed location — I wanted it to be a surprise. As we entered the rustic space, the smell of fresh wood shavings wafted around us. Our muscle-bound instructors greeted us and took us to a long room lined with wooden walls, targets, stumps of wood, and axes — dozens of axes, just waiting to be thrown. We were given lessons on safety and technique, and then we divided into teams and the games began. Have you ever thrown an ax at a target? It is a release. You feel the power as it flies from your grip; you feel the exhilaration when you hit the bullseye. We had a phenomenal time throwing the massive blades, and it, too, was a form of relaxation — a time to reflect upon the joy of being together, of giving thanks for the work we do, and for releasing stress in a kick-butt kind of way. We were rejuvenated, invigorated, and our purpose was validated; we were even more focused on our mission and purpose after that day.

Occupy yourself with that which soothes, strengthens, and supports you. Listen to joyful music, watch an uplifting movie, read a heartwarming story, create art. Spend time laughing with friends, watch a sunset from atop a roof. Throw an ax, pound a punching bag. Be still, and focus on the many blessings that fill our world. There is always goodness to be found. Life gives us twists and turns, and we need to find ways to stay the path along our journey.

Focus

As a member of Leadership Atlanta, I was honored to be selected for a special event: The Driven Women Experience at Porsche. I had looked forward to the opportunity for weeks, and when I finally walked out onto the track, my heart pounded in anticipation. My driving instructor, Chuck, met me and walked me over to a bright-red Porsche Targa. As he talked me through the speeding, curving, and swerving that would ensue, I could feel the adrenaline surging through me. The experience was even more than I had hoped for. I tested my limits on the track and navigated the twists and turns of the handling circuit — a driving playground of sorts. For one challenge, I even floored the gas pedal, speeding like a bullet until I was told to slam the breaks before hitting a barrier. But without a doubt, the most thrilling challenge was the wet, low-friction circle. A massive sea of cement was covered in water, and as I accelerated toward it, a kickplate — one of only three of its kind in the world — lifted from the ground, intentionally sending the car into a tailspin. The car went around and around in 360s while simultaneously sliding across the pavement. It was glorious. I was not scared; I was exhilarated. And I felt completely able to handle it. How? Well, Chuck had been a wonderful instructor, and the key lesson of the day had been consistent: Always keep your eyes and attention focused on where you want the car to go. Do not look to the left or right; always look to the place where you want to be, not where you are.

> ### Always look to the place where you want to be, not where you are.

As I drove back to school in the afterglow of the morning, Chuck's words stayed with me. So often, we allow ourselves to be preoccupied with things that distract us; we veer off track, and it weakens us by stealing our purpose and joy. There is power in being still — in taking time to meditate upon the direction we want our lives to take. In doing so, we are better able identify our purpose and fortify our steps toward achieving it. So many factors can cause us to change lanes, run out of gas, and even break down. But when we are able to focus on our purpose that lies ahead, we are more likely to get to our destination faster. When we occupy ourselves with unhealthy relationships, behaviors, lifestyles, thought patterns, and emotions, we tend to detour, or even worse, we crash and burn.

When you dream, what do you dream about? For over twenty years, I have had a recurring nightmare. I am driving in a pickup across expansive rolling plains. The sky turns a greenish hue, and oncoming tornadoes approach me from every angle. I stop the truck, and suddenly a two-year-old version of Madison is with me. I cradle her in my arms as I run looking for shelter, and when none can be found, I lie on the ground on top of her, trying with all of my might to protect her as pounding wind pummels me. I then awake, completely shaken. The dream has been a consistent one, but there is a pattern: it happens when I am overwhelmed and mentally and physically exhausted. I believe that perhaps it is God's way of telling me to slow down and be still; I cannot help others effectively if I cannot help myself. I must stop and breathe. When I do this, I am not only able to dream about things — I am also able to dream *for* them. My mind opens up to all of life's many possibilities and creativity is unleashed.

I also have a beautiful recurring dream; I have had it since I was a small girl. The setting always changes, but in the dream, I can fly. I take a running start, and I do a version of swimming in the air; I can feel the power of my arms and legs as I propel myself forward, eventually soaring over valleys, rivers, grasslands, and sometimes even the city on a starry night. I am empowered; I am free. When does this dream happen? During the times when I occupy myself with positive, purposeful thoughts and interactions; it happens when my soul is at rest.

There is so much clutter in the world — mixed messages about who or what we should be, how we should act, what we should have, and when we should have it. Many obstacles confuse, confound, control, and change us; they distract us from what we ultimately want to accomplish. Are you spending your time on making your dreams a reality? Are you taking care of yourself? Are you focusing on what is important to you? Or are you allowing life's distractions to lure you away from your greatest version of you? The good news is that you can get back on the road, but you must be able to learn to recognize and release that which no longer deserves to control your life.

There is an odd phenomenon about time: the older we become, the faster time seems to go. Think about it. The four years you were in high school probably seemed like an eternity, but perhaps the most recent four years sped by at a lightning pace. So, if time is so valuable, how are you going to invest it in your hopes, your dreams, your purpose? How will you occupy the time you have been given?

Have you ever had a song get stuck in your head? It can loop over and over, despite our efforts to shake it. Our thoughts are this way. If something is going to get stuck in your head, work to make it something positive. If you spend your time hurting others, engaging in unhealthy behaviors, or participating in harmful activities, then you are taking the precious gift of time and turning it into your enemy, not your friend. If you spend your time meditating on all that is wrong in your life, then you are not leaving time to focus on all that is right. If you are running yourself ragged and not taking time to recharge, then you are depleting your strength. If you are occupying your time loving things more than people, then you are creating emptiness. Do not allow yourself to be swallowed by such a vortex of negativity — intentionally seek joy instead.

Laugh

Perhaps one of the greatest ways to strengthen oneself is to look for the joy, even in the most unusual circumstances. I am going to share one story about my mama's passing, but this is a happy memory, not a sad one.

On the eve of my mother's funeral, I felt great sorrow; I was hollow. It was as if I were going through the motions, numb from the journey we had been through over the previous three years. Funeral visitations are necessary, but difficult. *Smile, nod, hug, shake hands, smile, nod, hug, shake hands. . . .* It is an endless loop of introductions, reunions, apologies, and condolences. Grief often comes in waves, and at one point, I felt the onset of a big, ugly cry coming on. I darted into the funeral parlor bathroom to gather myself, and then I saw them: the draperies. Long, black draperies patterned with large pink, green, and beige flowers. These were not just any draperies; they were draperies made from the *exact fabric as the dress I was wearing*. I kid you not. I could not stop laughing from the absurdity of it all. Here I was, trying to look elegant and classy, only to find that my dress was made of fabric from funeral parlor draperies. I howled with laughter through my tears — deep belly laughs as the droplets streamed down my face. My mama always loved a good laugh, and it was as if she were right there with me, letting me know that it would be okay. I swear she must have been the one who led me to buy that dress in the first place.

The irony was so wonderful that I had to find someone to show, or else no one would ever believe me. I swung open the door to find Ron standing in the hallway.

"Are you okay?" he asked. I must have looked half crazed, laughing through the tears that smeared my makeup.

"Come with me!" I said, grabbing his arm and pulling him right into the bathroom with me. I didn't have to say anything else — I just posed between the curtains and held them.

Joy in the midst
of sorrow

"Nooooo!" he laughed. "Noooo! Oh, my God! Kim, you are dressed in funeral home curtains!"

"I know!" I shrieked. "Isn't it wonderful?"

He snapped a photo that I will forever cherish — a reminder that even in the depths of sorrow, there is joy.

Researchers have found that when we laugh, we release endorphins that can help relieve some types of pain. We reduce stress hormones, and we can even increase antibody-producing cells. To put it simply, laughter is good for us. I am not talking about hurtful laughter that belittles another or inappropriate laughter that hurts someone. In the Modify chapter, I talked about the importance of changing our mindset and finding the positive. I reiterate it here with an emphasis upon laughter because laughter makes you healthier; it makes you stronger. Was it alright to laugh at my mother's funeral visitation? Absolutely. Did it mean I wasn't hurting or that I loved her less? On the contrary. I had never loved her more than I did at that moment. When we are able to find humor in the midst of chaos, it sometimes transforms life's stressors into the most joyful stories to remember. Laughter and gratitude fortify us; they keep us on course.

Such was the case when some of our staff stayed at what we now affectionately call the Murder Hotel. We were in Japan with our eighth-grade students, and before I go further, let me emphasize that we were in Japan! We were surrounded by warm, gracious people, and the magnitude of the opportunity was not lost upon any of us. After all, it is one of the most beautiful and peaceful places on earth. It is also one of the cleanest. Taxis have white linen covers on the passenger seats that are changed daily; there is absolutely no litter on the streets. Sidewalks sparkle; all public places are pristine.

After three days in Tokyo, we ventured by bullet train to Wakayama, where our students attended school and stayed in the homes of Japanese students. While our students enjoyed their homestays, we had lovely accommodations in Wakayama. On our second night there, however, our guide informed us that we would be changing hotels for one night due to a convention in town. We readily packed up and took taxis to the new address, admiring those linen seat covers again. However, we looked at one another quizzically when our tour guide drove away in his taxi; he had always stayed in the same hotel as us.

We entered a small, compact building and found ourselves in an even smaller room not much bigger than an elevator. A man sat chain-smoking behind a three-foot-long counter. In the corner was a card table with a sign that read *Shampoo Bar* in both Japanese and English. Atop it sat three bottles of shampoo with the little paper cups that are typically used for ketchup in fast food restaurants. The nine of us struggled to fit into the space, and as we assessed the situation, our eyes darted back and forth at one another. At this point, we weren't sure whether to laugh or cry.

Upon communicating to the receptionist that we didn't want to rent by the hour and that we did, indeed, plan on staying the night, he gave us our keys and pointed to the shampoo bar so that we could pump and take our daily allotment. As we walked single file down the narrow hallway that led to the elevators, we laughed and decided that everything would surely be fine once we got to the rooms. Two at a time we took our ascent to our respective floors since the elevators could not accommodate more of us.

When Kirk and I exited the elevator, we found Ben and Junior, eyes wide open and mouths agape. They were assessing what could only be described as a massive blood stain on the carpet; it was the in shape of a body. It appeared to have been there for a while, perhaps years, but it was still there nonetheless.

"Nooooo . . . is that . . . um . . ." I stammered.

"I think so," Ben replied.

I scanned the rest of the space and looked to a corner where there sat an even tinier table than the one downstairs. This time the sign said *Cleaning Supplies* and contained a blue liquid in a spray bottle, hand sanitizer, rubber gloves, and paper towels. My mind darted back to the fact that this place rented by the hour.

We looked at each other and burst into laughter — deep belly laughs that left us doubled over. What on Earth had we gotten ourselves into? The more we laughed, the more we laughed. We texted Susan, Camille, David, and J. the pictures of the body outlined on the floor; they sent us a picture of the cleaning supply table on their floor. Theirs had air freshener, too.

After we pulled it together, we decided to go to our rooms and look for other hotels online. I opened my door to find a bed that dipped into sink-hole; a faded bedspread had been haphazardly placed across it. There was one wooden chair in the corner. It is not uncommon for hotel rooms in other countries to be quite small, and this one was the width of the bed.

Then I made my tragic error — I could not help myself. I pulled back the bedspread and sheets to find rusty stains. Immediately I Googled bedbugs on my phone and saw that yes, they can leave rustlike stains on a mattress. Panicked, I sent photos in a GroupMe text to the others.

"Nooooo . . . ," texted Ben. "For the love of God, why would you do that?"

We all frantically started to search every online possibility for other rooms, but in the whole city, there was not one vacancy. The convention attendees had booked every single room. Well, the convention attendees and our guide, who was ignoring my frantic texts for help. We gathered in the street in front of the hotel and decided that we should just walk around the city because we surely couldn't sleep. We walked and laughed, walked and laughed until our feet could carry us no more. Everything was closed. I think we each hoped that a magical secret hotel would materialize before us, but none did. We returned to our hotel and asked the receptionist where the restaurant was that would provide our breakfast.

"Third floor," he said, "but it is not open until six in the morning."

We thanked him and headed down the hall. I said to Junior, "Are you thinking what I am thinking?"

"We are going to the third floor, y'all!" he said.

We figured we would sleep in the restaurant. It had to be cleaner. As we exited the third-floor elevators, we found expandable partitions that were locked. Okay . . . here is where you might judge me. I took a credit card, slid it between the partitions, and sort of, well, broke into the kitchen.

We spilled into the room and were so grateful for somewhere to sit — any-where to sit. It was more of a kitchenette than a restaurant, but we were desperate. The chairs were hard and wooden, and we put our heads down upon the small wooden tables. And then we laughed all over again. Honestly, we were exhausted, miserable, and a little loopy from the whole thing, but the hilarity of it all did not escape us.

Finally, in the middle of the night, one-by-one we returned to our rooms. I checked for moving bed bugs and saw none; I lay a towel on my bed, put a hood over my head, and prayed for the best as I fell into a fitful, two-hour sleep. In the morning, we were all awakened by J. Amezqua's text messages.

J., our talented photographer and hilarious friend, had snapped shots of himself in a tiny robe at the shampoo bar in the lobby. He was spreading shampoo in his dry hair while the horrified receptionist looked on in confusion. It was the perfect ending to a momentous night.

In the words of Dickens, "It was the best of times, it was the worst of times." We were miserable, yet we were overjoyed. We were exhausted, yet we were invigorated. We were horrified, yet we were tickled beyond words. How? We focused on the fact that we were blessed to be on a trip that others only dream of; we were fortunate to have one another. We fortified ourselves by seeing the humor in it all, and it made all the difference. Whenever we are together, if one of us just says, "Murder Hotel," we burst into deep belly laughs. It is a beautiful memory we will always cherish — one that made our bond stronger. Sometimes in life, no matter how much you prepare, things just go wrong. In those moments, we have to hunt for joy.

However, I fully recognize that sometimes we cannot find it, no matter how desperately we seek it.

Believe

We are created with potential beyond our understanding; we have a purpose bigger than we can comprehend. I have written this book for all people — those from various faiths and those with no faith at all. My wish is that no matter where you fall along that continuum, my words have given you hope, help, or healing. However, since I have shared my story with you, I would be omitting an important truth if I did not disclose how instrumental faith was in my own journey. My faith is my core that sustains me, and it is the lens through which I write and share my insights with you. It was faith that got me off of that closet floor; it was faith that pushed me to walk away and start anew. Faith gave me the courage to build RCA; faith led me to adopt my sons.

I believe that we are all spiritual beings, that we are created with a void that can only be filled with the belief in something greater than ourselves. Many try to fill it with other things — material possessions, money, drugs, alcohol, food,

I believe that we are all spiritual beings, that we are created with a void that can only be filled with the belief in something greater than ourselves.

relationships, fame, work, attention, thrill seeking—and while these things might give you happiness for a season, they often magnify the emptiness inside of us when they do not work. You do not have to believe what I believe, but my hope for you is that you believe in something. I want that for you. Seek out time to read, listen, and learn more about your spirituality. Consider it a quest—an adventure. It requires you to be still—something that is difficult in our fast-paced lives. However, if you want to know someone, you must spend time with them and talk to them. If you want to know your Creator, it is the same. Prayer doesn't have to be formal; talking to God can be like talking to a friend. In our darkest loneliness hours, we all need a friend, don't we?

Faith for me is not just a feeling—there have been many times in my life when God felt far away; there have been times I cried out to Him and asked Him where He was; there have been times when I shouted at Him in anger. I have questioned Him, and I have pushed Him away. I have never, however, stopped talking to Him, and for me, that has changed my life. Our lives will not ever be without pain and struggle—we are not promised perfection in a fallen world. I will not always understand life, but prayer has made me much better at living it. It empowers me, it guides me, it soothes me, it strengthens my core. It also helps me to understand the power of forgiveness.

Forgive

When someone hurts us deeply, the pain can consume us; it is all-encompassing. It festers and takes on a power of its own, seething within us like a vast chasm of despair. Left unattended, it grows more powerful and overtakes our ability to see things clearly. It seeps into our other relationships like an ever-present poison. Consequently, the person who hurt us continues to control our happiness; we cede our power to them. Even if the person is no longer in our lives.

As you have read about some of my experiences, you might have thought, *Well, Kim went through a rough time, but I have experienced far worse.* If this is the case, I am so sorry for your pain. Most definitely, we all know of people who have gone through circumstances that are beyond our comprehension, and we will never understand why they must endure such heartache.

I am blessed to have the opportunity to interact with so many educators each year, and many share their stories with me — stories of pain, agony, defeat, sickness, betrayal, abuse, loss, oppression, loneliness, and evil. Through their stories, they have taught me much about living and loving and surviving. Those who are fighters have often endured the most horrific circumstances of all, yet they still move forward. They continue to live and let the beauty of life continue to unfold. How?

They have taught me that to forgive someone, they do not have to deserve it. They did not have to earn it. However, if and when you are able to do it, you release the person's control over you and your future happiness. It is the greatest gift you give *yourself* because you no longer give that person the right to control your joy or your success. You empower yourself to heal, and the other person has no claim to your emotional well-being. It can take time; it can be the hardest thing you will ever do, but I wish that for you. There are times when you need to come together with the person who has hurt you and talk it out; there are times when you need to flee and never see or talk to that person again. But regardless of the scenario, one thing is necessary for your inner peace, and that is forgiveness.

When we have been wronged, it is easy to occupy our every waking moment with anger, rage, indignation, and sorrow. We cannot believe we have been betrayed; we do not understand how someone who cared about us

We don't have to understand to forgive.
Instead, we have to release to forgive.

could be so cold, selfish, dishonest, or cruel. But we don't have to understand to forgive. Instead, we have to release to forgive. If someone has wronged you and you find yourself allowing it to hijack your happiness, work on forgiving them, even if you do not want to do it. You don't have to even speak to them to do so . . . it is something that happens within you. You will feel lighter, and eventually the knots that bind you will be released. It does not mean that you do not fight for what is right; it does not mean that you do not stand up for yourself. It simply means that as you navigate the situation, your thoughts, words, and actions are not dictated by the rage and anger; your mind will be more focused upon insight, wisdom, and your purpose — something they can no longer take away from you. Surrendering to rage is a form of self-sabotage. It can steal our peace. It can even steal our dreams.

Honestly, sometimes I just don't feel like being helpful, good, noble, and true. Sometimes being selfish, angry, vengeful, catty, and spiteful looks far more appealing. However, surrendering to those emotions ultimately diminishes the spirit; it weakens the soul. Sometimes I would rather be lazy; other times I don't feel up to learning yet another thing. But sloth and ignorance certainly do not pay off in the long run. Sometimes I feel like the world will fall apart if I don't stop working so hard; however, I will fall apart if I do not take time to be still. Celebrate your body, edify your mind. Pray. Appreciate. Surrender to emotions that soothe your soul, soften your sorrow, and strengthen your spirit. In doing so, you will be fortified to step into your purpose with unwavering resolve and focused fury — the fortitude of a fighter.

Notes

♪ When we fortify ourselves, we are better able to fulfill our purpose and passion.
♪ We have to strengthen ourselves to be strong for others.
♪ Do not take our physical capabilities for granted; if you can move, move often.
♪ We should engage in activities that activate and sharpen the mind.
♪ Our minds can continue to grow throughout our lifetime.
♪ No matter how old you are, take opportunities to learn and grow.

♪ Our input affects our output and our ability to uplift, serve, live, laugh, and love.

♪ Occupying our thoughts with negative emotions can consume and even break us.

♪ Set aside opportunities to reflect upon gratitude — it will enrich your life.

♪ When we occupy our mind with positive influences, we affect our ability to handle obstacles.

♪ Focus on the place where you want your life to be.

♪ Laughter reduces stress and can enrich our lives

♪ We are spiritual beings. Seek time to be still and embrace your spirituality.

♪ To forgive someone, they don't have to deserve it or earn it. When we forgive, it is a gift we give ourselves.

Change Your Tune

♪ Make it a priority to move, run, jump — use the gift of your physical body each and every day.

♪ Try something new to continue challenging your mind. Learn a language, play an instrument, read more, listen more. Keep challenging your mind in ways that will help you be a lifelong learner.

♪ Embrace the power that gratitude has upon your well-being. Take gratitude walks, keep a journal, make lists of things for which you are grateful.

♪ Avoid distractions and remain focused on that which is noble, good, honorable, and true in pursuit of your dreams.

♪ Don't take small setbacks so seriously. See the humor and joy, even in difficult situations.

♪ Find time to be still and connect with your spirituality. Seek answers to questions you may have, but approach spiritual growth with the same diligence as your physical and mental well-being.

♪ Identify people whom you need to forgive, and work to release the bitterness, anger, and pain that you hold within you. Write down your thoughts and feelings if it helps you process them — try writing a letter that you don't even have to send.

Identify
Modify
Amplify
Unify
Fortify

chapter 6

Battle Cry

Sometimes our only options are to give up
or to dig deep and push through. We must release
our BATTLE CRY and fight with
everything that is within us.

———————

2018 It is a sunny November day, and as I finish my long walk, I open
the mailbox to find three matching envelopes from USCIS,
United States Citizenship and Immigration Services. My hands shake
as I open them, praying that they contain three green cards. Instead, there
are three formal letters, each identical. I frantically read them twice, hoping
that the text on the pages will change and that I have somehow read it all
wrong. The letters contain RFIs — requests for more information. They
state that I have not accurately proven that my sons' birth parents still

live in South Africa. I am confused by this. Where else would they be? Wait — do they think that they are somehow illegally living here?

Do they not realize that my sons are my children? The boys are legally adopted, and they have been living with us for over five years! Holding my hand over my mouth, I try to swallow the panic rising within me as I continue reading. It gets worse: I have thirty days to submit proof of their birth parents' residence in South Africa.

Immediately, my head begins to race; thoughts swirl into a vortex of confusion and anxiety. Trembling, I rush into the house to show Scotty the letters. He attempts to calm me and proceeds to call our attorney to schedule a meeting for the next morning. I sleep fitfully, constantly reminding myself to relinquish the fears that threaten my ability to think clearly.

Finally, I get out of bed. One by one, I enter each son's room and watch each sleep. I say a prayer for protection, for guidance, for wisdom. And with each room I enter, I grow stronger and more determined. After closing the last bedroom door, I sit at the top of the stairs and stare out the large window at the twinkling stars in the dark night sky. Calm washes over me; I know what I must do. What any mother would do. I must go into battle for my sons.

Sometimes, despite our efforts to do everything right, we are still knocked off our feet, battered and bruised beyond normal boundaries. Sometimes, situations leave us backed into a corner, and our only options are to give up or to dig deep and push through. We want to crumble on the closet floor, but we must continue living, breathing, and battling our brokenness. In such times, we must find the tiniest of sparks within us and fan them into flames; we must release our battle cry and fight with everything that is within us — not only for ourselves, but also for the ones we love. The strengths we have identified, the behaviors we have modified, and the purpose we have amplified give us the fortification to burst forward into action.

One cannot apply for US citizenship for an international adoption like ours for two years, and I fully understand this. After our sons were adopted, we immediately visited several immigration attorneys to find the best one to help us handle the intricacies of our case. We methodically documented everything that was necessary, and over the course of several months, we acquired hundreds of pages of proof of our relationship with our sons, our familial bonds, our abundant love for them. We submitted hundreds of family photos, dozens of letters from friends, family, and coworkers, and bank and credit card records showing every single transaction on their behalf. We sent school records, church records, health records, home study records, adoption records, and their new birth certificates. I prayed over those pages, and then our attorney sent them in, letting us know we should plan to wait months before hearing anything. We were encouraged when our boys received documentation in the mail that would enable them to work legally in the United States, but what we really needed was for our sons to receive their green cards, granting them permanent legal residence in the United States. Once green cards were acquired, we could then apply for their US citizenship.

So, on that fateful day when the RFI letters arrived in my mailbox, I was devastated. We had already provided every conceivable document, and I knew firsthand how hard it would be to get more. This whole process had already taken years, and yet I had thirty days to prove what seemed impossible to prove. However, if I did not, my boys . . . my children . . . my beloved sons could be deported, despite the fact that they were legally adopted. I could not let this happen.

As we sat in the attorney's office, she detailed an extensive list of additional documents we would try to obtain from South Africa. "It will be difficult to get all of these, especially with such limited time."

"I will get them myself. I am going to South Africa," I replied.

My attorney said, "You are going to fly all the way to South Africa in hopes of gathering these documents?"

"Yes," I replied. "I will leave this weekend."

Scotty answered, "She is pretty determined. If she says she will get the documents, I know she will."

"Okay, then," my attorney said, nodding and smiling.

I used every SkyMile I had saved from years of giving speeches to get my ticket, and one week later, I was on a plane to South Africa, fighting for my sons' future. Scotty needed to stay home with the boys — they could not travel outside the country until we had those green cards. I reassured Scotty that I would be fine on my own since I had traveled there so many times with RCA. However, my big brother Stephen, a retired firefighter, insisted on going with me, and I accepted his gracious offer.

I had met Sisipho's birth parents and Sabelo's birth mother before adopting the boys; Sabelo's father was deceased. I had never met Phakamani's mother in person — she lived in the shacks of Cape Town, hundreds of miles from Soweto. We had posted notices of Phakamani's pending adoption in South African newspapers in an attempt to locate his birth father, but he was never found. None of the parents had mailing addresses. Their email was unreliable, and they were not always able to access it. How do you find a paper trail for those who pay a few rand a month to live in a garage or a spare room for which no receipts are issued? How do you prove that someone who has lived in a shack for thirteen years is, in fact, a resident of South Africa? What if the phones are prepaid and there are no bills or records of payments? What if employment has been spotty or nonexistent? My attorney had given me a list of things to seek — receipts, legal documents, bills . . . anything that could show South African residence. She encouraged me to focus on getting affidavits from other South African citizens who would verify that they knew the birth parents and that they had, in fact, always lived there. For most of the seventeen-hour flight, I planned and prayed. My hands sometimes trembled, my heart raced, but I convinced myself that there is nothing like a mother's love. I would prevail.

Arthur, our guide for school trips, met me at the airport with Aubrey, a driver who would help me on the journey. Arthur arranged for me to connect with the birth parents; they were willing to help however they could. Giving their children up for adoption had been an act of love, not abandonment. I cannot imagine the sacrifices they felt they had to make for their children's well-being; I cannot comprehend how hard that must have been for them.

I learned that in South Africa affidavits are provided by police stations. In a constant stream, Aubrey and I transported people who knew the birth parents to various police stations all over Soweto to give their sworn statements. I obtained letters from places where the parents had been employed over the years and certificates from training classes they had taken. I found church records and minutes from church meetings where they were present. I scanned photos of ID badges, delivery notices, and photos. I convinced stores to let me scan evidence of clothing put on layaway; I found records of old bank statements. I went to the schools the boys' younger siblings had attended and made copies of the records. From sun up until after midnight each day, I was focused on my quest for information, for evidence, for truth. God showed up.

We then flew to Cape Town where I found and met Phakamani's birth mom, Kwiri, for the first time. She lived in the shacks — thousands upon thousands of makeshift tin structures that were interconnected for miles. Just blocks away from the shacks sits downtown Cape Town, one of the most beautiful cities in the world. The juxtaposition of the extreme wealth against the abject poverty angered me, for it was colonization and apartheid that had caused such stark disparities. Kwiri had lived in the shacks for thirteen years; her tin structure was painted bright purple in an attempt to create beauty amid the shambles. Plastic milk jugs crowded her cramped space; she filled them with dishwashing liquid and diluted them with water to sell for a profit. Power lines were rigged haphazardly to give her electricity, and water stains ran down her walls, due to the holes in her roof. Yet, she is a fighter. She laughs boldly like Phakamani, and I instantly loved her.

Kwiri had given birth to Phakamani as a young girl. She was unable to raise him, but she had done her very best to survive. She had taken courses in everything from power tool cleaning to data collection in the hope of making herself employable. She had proudly saved every course certificate, and each contained the dates of the classes. I figured out how to get them notarized, giving thanks for her diligence. In Cape Town, we obtained more affidavits; I found bank records. Kwiri had a small refrigerator in her shack; I was able to obtain the delivery receipt. We went to the offices where Kwiri had applied for subsidized housing thirteen years ago and found paperwork showing that she was still on the waiting list. Kwiri's strength and interminable spirit will forever leave an imprint on my heart.

My Phakamani
(photo by J. Amezqua)

Throughout my journey, and despite the struggles I observed in South Africa, there was hope, strength, and love. Most important, there was gratitude. Thanks were given for every meal, every opportunity, and every moment spent with loved ones. Thanks were given for shelter and every basic need. There was laughter and song and faith that transcended the circumstances. And this faith was what I clung to as I continued to fight to get the job done for my sons.

I carried every document I found in my backpack everywhere I went, clutching it tightly to my stomach. I scanned every single one, I saved every single one, I emailed every single one. I wanted there to be multiple copies so that nothing could be lost; those pages were more precious to me than gold. A legion of people back home was praying for me, and it was as if each page was delivered by angels who led the way. At night, I would collapse in the bed and sob, from exhaustion, fear, relief, and gratitude; my tears cleansed me of anxiety and replaced it with truth, hope, strength, and purpose. My big brother Stephen was there to offer comfort, just like he had always done when we were little. I was grateful that I had agreed to let him help; his presence was an additional source of strength.

We flew back to Johannesburg for a final day before departing, and I had one last stop: I had promised to visit Sabelo's great-grandmother back in Soweto. As I approached, she hobbled toward me, wiping her hands on her apron. I reached out my arms for a hug, and she tightly embraced me for several moments before we sat down. I told her stories about Sabelo — how smart he was, how strong, how good. I showed her photos. I shared my journey and why I was there. She said very few words, but she nodded and listened. There was a quiet strength about her; she exuded wisdom and peace. As I spoke, her deep gaze penetrated my eyes . . . she looked through them and into my soul. When she finally spoke, she said, "I can see God behind you. He is here with you." Goosebumps rose on my arms, and I embraced her for several moments before finally departing.

After nine days in Soweto, I returned and delivered the papers directly to my attorney. Five days after that, they were organized, catalogued, and arranged to present to USCIS. There was nothing else we could do but wait. Once again, my attorney told me it could take a year to hear anything.

Two months later, I went to my mailbox again to find another set of letters from USCIS. My hands trembled uncontrollably as I carefully opened one, then another, then the third. Tears spilled down my cheeks. Then I screamed, I shouted, I leapt, and I ran into the house to share the good news, forgetting that no one was inside. I ran back outside and found Scotty doing yardwork in the back of our lot. I waved the paperwork in the air and ran while yelling, "They are here! They were approved! We got the green cards!" He thought something terrible had happened until he came closer and heard what I was actually saying. He threw his arms around me and held me for several minutes as I sobbed it all out.

Moments later, Sabelo returned, and I saw him in the driveway. I ran again, shouting, "You have been approved! You are a permanent legal resident! We did it!" Sabelo lifted me in a bear hug, swung me around, and laughed and laughed with pure joy.

"You did it. I can't believe you did it. Thank you, thank you," he repeated again and again.

Visiting Cape Town, 2019
(photo: J. Amezqua)

My sons consider the United States to be home, yet they can now freely travel the world to see all of its majesty and wonder. They can also visit the country of their birth. Two months after receiving those green cards, Scotty and I took them to South Africa to reconnect with their ancestral land and with loved ones who rejoiced upon their return. Almost one year later, my beloved sons were finally sworn in as US citizens. When they are older, my sons plan to use their educations, resources, and talents to help make changes for the beautiful people of Soweto; they are dedicated to giving back to the land of their childhood.

Push

When I had told some people that I was going to go to South Africa, they said that it was a lot to do and that it probably would just work out without going to such great lengths. Perhaps it would have, but perhaps not. While I believe that God answers prayers, I also believe that we have a responsibility to act, to move, to step out on faith, to push, to dig deep, to go into battle with all that we are. Sabelo's great-granny had verified that God was behind me, but I believe He was there to push me forward, not to let me sit still. I had to get on that plane and do what needed to be done. Period.

When you are in battle, listen to those who are willing to fight with and for you, not those who work to try to discourage you. I chose to listen to those who said, "You go, Mama! Beautiful! Yes — go and get what you need. You will find it!" Those are the people whose words guided me — the encouragers, the supporters, the believers. They had faith in me, and as my dear friend Ben said, "Of course you found what you needed. I never doubted for a moment that you would."

I did. I doubted when I lay in bed at night, overcome with fear for my sons' futures. And I fully recognize my privilege here: I was able to get a phenomenal attorney who could help me; I was able to find the resources to go to South Africa to find what I needed; I had family and friends to support me along the journey. There are many in life who face battles without resources, without support, without knowledge of where to even begin. But for all of us, when we are in the depths of those hours, it is more important than ever to fight, to get up, to move forward, to push through. We cannot give up; we must forge ahead and use every bit of strength left within us.

> ## The human spirit is indomitable; we are created to outlast and survive, despite our circumstances.

The human spirit is indomitable; we are created to outlast and survive, despite our circumstances. It is far easier said than done, but sometimes survival is itself the victory for that day. We all know individuals who have experienced unfathomable heartache far worse than mine; we have met people who have faced loss or death that is without comprehension. We do not know how they move forward, but they do. They find purpose, they resolve themselves to keep living, loving, and breathing. They teach us all that it is our duty to do the same.

Dig

When we are faced with seemingly insurmountable challenges, we must dig — we must access that part deep in our souls that holds the fire of a warrior, the strength of a fighter. But how? By delving into our past and remembering how we have risen from the ashes before.

Whenever doubts seep into my consciousness, I stop and reflect upon times when things seemed completely impossible to endure, yet in the end, they came together. I survived. And you will, too.

- Do you remember a time when you thought you could not go on, but you did?
- Was there a time when you thought things were so broken they could never be repaired, but they were?
- Can you remember a situation or obstacle that hurt so much that it took your breath away, but now it is but a distant memory?

How did you get off that closet floor . . . out of that bed . . . and walk boldly back into life?

You rose up . . . and you will do it again. You were overwhelmed, but you overcame. You were battered, but you healed. You were shattered, yet you mended. You felt like you had no options, but you found a solution. You were alone, yet you found support. You had given up on yourself, but you learned to believe in yourself and find faith again. You were broken into a million pieces, yet you emerged whole; you were stronger than ever before.

Those challenging experiences have composed the notes of your life's melody — they are the verses of your battle cry, your fight song. Use them to identify your truth, modify your mindset, and amplify your purpose. Let them crescendo to fortify your spirit and unify you with those who support you and celebrate your power, passion, peace, and purpose.

Build

We pulled up to the condemned factory and jumped out of the car. Tangled barbed wire clung to broken fencing; torn awnings dangled from bent fragments of aluminum frames. Collapsing structures hugged one another as if they were holding each other upright. We were in one of the highest crime zones in the city, and as we tiptoed over strewn litter to enter the lot, the real estate agent shook his head and said, "I am sorry—this is no place for a school."

Ron and I looked at the dilapidated brick building—the crumpling annexed structures, the dirt lot that was punctuated by shards of glass, nails, lumber, and trash. Ron smiled at me, and I smiled and nodded in return.

"We'll take it!" we both exclaimed in unison.

This was the place where we chose to build the Ron Clark Academy, a school that we dreamed would be unlike any other. We chose the space because we wanted to show that there is potential in everything and that we can create magic in the most unlikely places if we only look for it. From amid the rubble and debris, we built a school filled with beauty, wonder, love, and laughter—a place that has impacted countless lives.

We saw something in the building others hadn't seen—we identified its worth. We modified the structure and made changes where necessary so that it would enable us to affect more students and educators, thus amplifying its purpose. We sought help from the community and unified ourselves with a team of amazing people for support. We fortified ourselves with knowledge, wisdom, and faith so we could push through, dig deep, and step into our life's purpose. Not only did Ron Clark help me build a school; he helped me rebuild my life.

If such miracles can come from a shattered, broken building, imagine how many more miracles can emerge from a shattered, broken spirit. For it is people, not things, who really breathe magic and life into this world. Unfortunately, it takes more than the wave of a wand to do so. The magic in our lives must be built—step by step, brick by brick, day by day. It takes time. But from the depths of darkness and debris, we can build wonder, joy, breath, and life.

From the depths of darkness and debris, we can build wonder, joy, breath, and life.

As I have shared my stories with you, it is my hope that I have not made it sound like every obstacle was quickly tied up with a neat little bow. It took months — even years — to clean up much of the wreckage that had occurred. But with each passing day, I continued to build — not walls, but structures that contained windows and doors so the light could shine through, casting love, grace, joy, and hope upon the shadows. I wish the same for you. In fact, I wrote this for you.

Sing

I recently had a revelation while looking at a photo of my family.

If you had shown me this photo at age twenty-four and told me this would be my family at age fifty-four, I would have been completely confused, and when you began to explain it all to me, I most likely would not have believed you.

Who is *that man in the photo? Wait — I am married to someone else? Was I widowed? Divorced? What happened? Did the man I originally married hurt me? What did he do to me? What happened to him? Am I okay? Did I do something wrong?*

This new man is so handsome, but where did he come from? What is our story? Does he really love me? How did we meet? What is our life like together? What is his name?

And wait — are those three boys his sons somehow? Surely, they are not his biological kids . . . or mine . . . or is that even possible? Where did they come from? Are they my sons? Look at those beautiful faces. What is their story? Are they adopted? Who are they? How did this even happen? We look so happy together . . .

Is that my precious Madison? She grew up to be so beautiful. (How did all of this affect her? Is she okay? Is she happy? What is her life like now?)

Do I have a new last name? What is it?

What on earth happened to create this family? I cannot even imagine a logical explanation.

Yes, this photo brings me unfathomable joy and gratitude, but if you had shown it to me at twenty-four, I honestly would have freaked out. Why? Because it was not the picture I had painted for myself. In my imagination, I had my whole life planned out; I thought I knew just how everything should and would unfold. But my reality is far more beautiful than anything my limited imagination ever could have created. When I stop to think about how God wove the despair, delight, sorrow, and satisfaction together to create my life's tapestry, I stand in awe. Life still has heartache, grief, and pain, but blessings abound despite the struggles. Perhaps a picture of your current life does not bring you joy; perhaps your heart is breaking. Understand that there is more of your song still to be written; the lyrics will unfold as you hurt, heal, struggle, and succeed.

Growing older is both frustrating and fulfilling. Your skin wrinkles, your body aches, and your memory sometimes lapses. But those crinkles around your eyes? They are joy scars. Those body aches? They are the result of a life filled with running, jumping, climbing, and dancing. Those memory lapses? They occur when we have so many memorable experiences to store in our minds that they sometimes merge or hide. With age comes insight and the blessing of knowing how some of life's most painful plots were resolved. We finally get to see how the seeds we planted produced fruit; we learn how the pressure in our lives formed the diamonds.

If I had not endured brokenness, I never would have felt so whole. When we imagine our futures, we have an image of what we think our best lives should look like, but what we envision is often very limited. We fail to understand that there must be darkness in order to have light. We cannot fully understand joy if we have not ever experienced sorrow; we cannot fully comprehend love without heartbreak; we cannot fully understand the appreciation of receiving unless we have experienced not having. From the deepest hollows, joy can spring forth, crescendoing into a magnificent symphony . . . a fight song . . . *your* fight song. It is within you — it always has been. Do you hear it? Let it billow and surge within you; let it flow through you and echo across a world in need of your significance.

Remember that it is the valleys of our lives that make the ascent to the mountaintops all the more glorious to behold. Rise up and step into the depth and breadth of your power as you boldly proclaim your worth and your purpose. Let no one silence you. Sing it now, my friend.

The world is waiting to hear you.

Sing it now.

Notes

♪ Even when we do everything right, we can still be broken and defeated.

♪ In life's most difficult moments, we must release our battle cry and fight with all that we are.

♪ We have a responsibility to act, move, and step out on faith.

♪ We should listen to those who encourage, support, and believe in us.

♪ We must draw strength from reflecting upon ways that we have overcome challenges before.

♪ The human spirit is indomitable, and we are created to survive.

♪ There might be a better version of your life than the one you imagined for yourself.

♪ It is the valleys in our lives that help us better comprehend the blessings.

♪ There is a song within you that is waiting to be sung. Sing it now.

Change Your Tune

♪ When you feel that you cannot go on, keep pushing, striving, moving, breathing, and living. Choose living over existing; remember that you were created to be a survivor.

♪ Create a community that nourishes your growth: meet in a small group weekly and use the book study questions in the following section to identify, thrive, and connect to your true purpose. You can be the one that unifies the group.

♪ Reflect and record situations from your lifetime where you have overcome, pushed through — moments when you thought you could not go on, but you did. Celebrate and give thanks for the strength you had and use it to empower you through this current storm.

♪ Trust that the picture you paint for yourself is in no way as magnificent as the one that is awaiting you. Find ways to give thanks and reflect upon the journey, for you have already shown you have the strength for anything that comes your way.

♪ Know that others believe in you. I believe in you, too.

Book Study Questions

The following questions are designed to help you dig deeper into the text. I encourage you to use *Fight Song* for a book study with your friends or colleagues. Tag me at @kimbearden, and let me know how it goes!

Chapter 1: Identify

1. What are some of the factors that cause you the most stress at work? What factors are causing stress for your coworkers?
2. What are some of the biggest stressors in your personal life?
3. Do you believe that, if you just try harder, life will be without challenges? Why or why not?
4. How do you let your image of yourself affect your response to life's stressors?
5. What traits do you admire in other people? Do you see any of these traits in yourself?
6. What valuable qualities do you possess? List them.
7. Do you tend to be critical of yourself, or do you grant yourself grace? Why?
8. List some of the self-defeating language you have been telling yourself using "I'm just . . ." statements. Now rewrite your "I'm just . . ." statements as positive "I am . . ." statements.
9. How does identifying your gifts and talents lead to appreciation?
10. Was there a time when you didn't step into your own spotlight, potential, or greatness? Why?
11. Are you a worrier? Share some things that you worried about that never came to fruition.
12. List some negative "What if . . ." statements that we often tell ourselves.

Now, rewrite them as positive "What if . . ." statements instead. How can this empower you?

13. How do society and the media make us feel like we aren't enough?
14. Share some examples of unhealthy comparisons you have made between yourself and others.
15. Perfection is an illusion. Share with others the ways that we are held to this standard and how it can be detrimental.
16. Do you seek perfection from other people? Why or why not?
17. Can we really have it all? How do you define *it all*?
18. What does it mean to you to be all in? How are some ways that you can be more fully present?
19. What things make people jealous? How do you release that?
20. Discuss the difference between wants and needs and list some examples.
21. For individual reflection: What is your truth?

Chapter 2: Modify

1. Share some examples of when you allowed minor setbacks to dictate your happiness. How could you have modified your mindset in that situation?
2. Share examples of when a modified mindset made the situation a much better experience.
3. How can changing your mindset change your outlook and ability to handle stress?
4. What are some of your greatest fears?
5. What steps can you take to overcome them?
6. Do you believe that fear can keep us from achieving our purpose? Why or why not?
7. Have you ever missed an opportunity to achieve a dream or goal because of fear? If you could go back, how would you handle it differently?
8. How do you know when to take a leap or when to wait? Does peace play a factor in your decision?
9. Have you ever known someone whose bad decisions continued to affect their happiness and success? Without disclosing the person's name, share how modified behaviors might have changed the outcome.

10. If you feel comfortable sharing with the group, tell about a time that your behavior resulted in a poor outcome. What did you need to change? Note: If your situation involved poor communication, then check out my book *Talk to Me!*

11. What lies do we often tell ourselves to justify our behaviors? How about to justify others' behaviors?

12. Individually, write and reflect upon "Things would be better if . . ." statements. Meditate on ways to make some of them a reality.

Chapter 3: Amplify

1. Share a time when you were inspired by someone doing something for others. Why were you inspired?

2. Although some of life's most beautiful acts of kindness are done in private, share some with the group. When was a time that you did something for someone else just because you felt led to do so?

3. How do you feel when you do things for others? When do you resent it? When does it make your heart sing?

4. Sometimes when we try to help, things don't go as planned. What can we learn when this happens?

5. Do you believe that helping others when we are hurting can actually help us heal? Why or why not?

6. How can we use our own stories to help others who are hurting? Can you provide an example of when you were able to do this?

7. For you, what does it mean to seek significance? How can it amplify your purpose?

8. List some simple things that you or your group can do to uplift others. How can you make some of these things happen?

9. How can we live our lives so that we leave our mark, our legacy, upon this world?

Chapter 4: Unify

1. Share a memory of when you were surrounded by people who were special to you. Where were you? How did you feel? How did it affect you?
2. How does connecting with others strengthen us?
3. It is okay to find time for ourselves, but what can be the negative effects of isolating ourselves for too long?
4. What does it mean to build walls versus bridges? Which do you do? Why?
5. What are some helpful ways to build bonds and relationships with one another? Your students? Your family? Your coworkers?
6. When seeking meaningful relationships, what kind of people do you look for? Why?
7. Are you that kind of person in return? Why or why not?
8. Do you think that you do your part to nurture relationships? Why or why not? Is there something you need to change?
9. How can you foster more meaningful relationships with people who are different than you? What do you hope to learn from them? How can they enrich your life?
10. How can you learn more about others who have walked a different path? Why should you?

Chapter 5: Fortify

1. Think about how often you move. Do you walk, run, dance — do you find ways to stay active? What are some initial actions you can take to promote regular activity?
2. How can you incorporate more movement into your time with your students, your friends, or your family?
3. What would make you feel physically stronger? How can you make that happen?
4. How can you find ways to get more sleep? Live a healthier lifestyle?
5. Discuss some hobbies or activities that you do to strengthen your mind.
6. Is there something you have always wanted to learn how to do, such as learn a language or play an instrument or paint with oils? How can you make that happen?

7. What are additional ways that you can continue to learn and grow?
8. How do you think that our input affects our output?
9. How can you incorporate more gratitude? Make a list of things for which you are grateful. Do it individually and as a group.
10. Take a short gratitude walk with your group members and share your thoughts as you walk. Then do one alone sometime this week.
11. How does it help to keep our focus on what lies ahead instead of what distracts us?
12. Share a time when your soul felt at peace and at rest. What made it so? How can you have more moments like that?
13. Do you have any recurring dreams? Nightmares? What happens in them? What triggers them?
14. How can you declutter your mind with conflicting messages?
15. Share your best relaxation methods with your group.
16. Share a time when laughter made a terrible situation much better.
17. Discuss ways to incorporate more laughter into your workday, your classes, your life.
18. How does your spirituality affect your well-being? How can you make time to make it a priority?*
19. Do you believe that forgiveness is a gift you give yourself? Why or why not?
20. Individually, reflect upon people whom you have forgiven and those you have yet to forgive. If you feel comfortable, share with one another.

Chapter 6: Battle Cry

1. Do you know of someone who defeated the odds and overcame extreme adversity? Share what you learned from them.
2. Was this person you? Tell about a time you had to dig deep and push through a difficult time. What gave you strength to do so?

---

* Spirituality is very personal and might be something that you cannot discuss in some organizations. If it is discussed, it should be done in a way that shows respect for all viewpoints and perspectives. This question could be a silent, written reflection that is just done individually.

3. What things matter the most to you? For what things will you fight with all your might?
4. Whom do you listen to when you are dealing with difficult circumstances? Whom do you trust and why?
5. Do you think we are designed to be survivors? Why or why not?
6. If you could have seen your life today ten years ago, what would you have thought? Twenty years ago? Share examples of how the picture you imagined for yourself turned out to be different from the reality.
7. What is better than you imagined? What do you need to change, and how can you do it?
8. You are strong, you are fierce, you are able. Tell everyone in your group why. Then tell one another what you see in them.

Acknowledgments

To my husband, Scotty: You are my rock and my calm in the storm; you are the love of my life. Thank you for believing in me, supporting me, and loving me.

To my daughter, Madison: You are my warrior, my fighter, my sunshine, my mini-me, my joy. We made it, sweetheart. We did it. I love you with all that I am.

To my sons, Sisipho, Sabelo, and Phakamani: You are my very heartbeat, and I cannot imagine my world without you in it. Thank you for filling my life with incomprehensible joy and inspiration. You make me so proud, and I love you.

To my daddy, Jack Driscoll: You are the one who taught me the meaning of unconditional love. You are the world's best daddy, and I love you so very much. Thank you for always believing in me.

To my precious mother in heaven: I love and miss you so much, Mama. I hope that I continue to make you proud.

To my brothers, Bobby and Stephen Driscoll: It is wonderful to know that no matter what happens in life, you will always have my back. You taught me to be fierce and strong. You were the first to teach me to be a fighter. I love you.

To Linda, Rhonda, Jennifer, and Beth: Thank you for being my precious, loyal friends through thick and thin. You mean the world to me.

To the phenomenal staff of the Ron Clark Academy:

Kenneth Adams	Camryn Bradley
Jeffrey J. Amezqua	Kirk Brown
Joey Barr	Renita Burns
Junior Bernadin	Nadia Chochol
Michael Bonner	Ron Clark
Yolanda Boyd	Korey Collins

Tyrel Cooper
Cer'Princeton Harden
Pamela Haskins
Dr. Camille Jones
Jordan Jones-Wright
Diane Kemp
Troy Kemp
Dasia Kirkley
Dr. Yvette Ledford
Rhonda Lokey
Hutch McMillan
Tully Murray
Adejah Parrish

Chrissi Pepitone
Aujahuna Smith
David Spearman
Jai Springs
Daniel Thompson
Elektra Thompson
Alejandro Uria
Kyle Walcott
Benjamin Walker
Carrie-Jo Wallace
Aungelita Williams
Da'Nall Wilmer

. . . and all those who came before you. I am so grateful to call you my family. Thank you for your love, laughter, hard work, and dedication. You are extraordinary human beings, and you inspire me to do more, be more, and give more each and every day. I love you.

To J. Amezqua: Thank you for taking the photos for this book and for capturing so many of RCA's most precious moments with your camera lens. You are a genius.

To the Board of Trustees of the Ron Clark Academy: Thank you for sharing your time, talents, and resources with us. Your dedication and support help us transform countless lives, and I am forever grateful.

To Duane Ward, Ryan Giffen, and the rest of the team at Premiere Speakers Bureau: It has been an honor to be represented by you for the past nineteen years. Thank you for providing me with the opportunity to speak to thousands of educators around the world. I greatly appreciate all that you have done for RCA and for me.

To Dave and Shelley Burgess: Thank you for giving educators a voice so that we can work together to change the world. You support so many, and I am honored to be on your team.

To my amazing, beloved students, past and present: You have blessed me beyond measure, and you give my life purpose. I am better because of you, and I love you all.

To the past and present parents of RCA, especially my beloved mamas: You make me a better woman, a better mother, a better teacher, and a better human being. Thank you for the love you give.

And to Ron Clark: Not only did you help me to build a school, you helped me build a life. I am forever grateful. I love you, my friend.

About the Author

Kim Bearden is the cofounder, executive director, and a language arts teacher at the highly acclaimed Ron Clark Academy, an innovative middle school and educator-training facility in Atlanta. Each year, more than fifteen thousand educators from around the world visit RCA's classrooms and attend their workshops to learn better ways to engage students, promote academic rigor, and create a climate and culture that promotes success.

In 2016, Kim was honored at the White House for being inducted into the National Teachers Hall of Fame. She was selected from over seventy thousand nominations to be honored as the Disney American Teacher Awards Outstanding Middle School Humanities Teacher. The Milken Family Foundation selected her to receive the Award for Excellence in Education. She is the winner of the InfluencHer Award, the University of Georgia Outstanding Educator Award, and the Turknett Character Award for Servant Leadership. Women Works Media Group has named her one of Georgia's Most Powerful and Influential Women. Mercedes Benz named her a 2017 Greatness Lives Here recipient.

Over the past thirty-three years, she has been a teacher, instructional lead teacher, curriculum director, school board member, staff development trainer, and middle school principal. Kim is a bestselling author of two books, *Crash Course: The Life Lessons My Students Taught Me* and *Talk to Me: Find the Right Words to Inspire, Encourage, and Get Things Done*, by DBC Books.

Kim resides in a suburb of Atlanta with her husband, Scotty, and her three sons, Sisipho, Sabelo, and Phakamani. Her married daughter, Madison, and son-in-law, Taylor, live close by.

To learn more about Kim, follow her on social media.

Instagram: @kimbearden

Twitter: @kimbearden

Facebook: @kimbeardeneducator

or

Visit her website at kimbearden.com.

Invite Kim Bearden to Your Next Professional Development Event

Kim has delivered hundreds of keynote addresses and workshops to school districts, corporations, faith-based groups, leadership organizations, and women's conferences around the world. To book Kim to speak at your next event, contact Premiere Speakers Bureau at www.premierespeakers.com.

Kim's keynotes and workshops can be tailored to fit your organization's specific needs. However, some of her most requested presentations include the following:

Talk to Me: Find the Right Words to Inspire, Encourage, and Get Things Done
Through the use of stories and scenarios, Kim Bearden will share six principles for effective communication that will strengthen any organization's climate and culture. You will leave empowered with tools that will help you develop rapport, gain respect, support others, engage listeners, develop insight, and increase productivity!

Fight Song: Six Steps to Passion, Power, Peace, and Purpose
Kim will focus on ways to overcome feeling overwhelmed, overworked, and underappreciated. Through the use of her own personal journey and how she overcame tragedy, betrayal, heartbreak, and pain, Kim will help audience members realize their influence and strength. Her six principles will leave participants feeling empowered and ready for any challenges they face.

Creating a Climate and Culture for Success

Kim will motivate, inspire, and remind participants of the powerful impact they can have despite the pressures and challenges of their profession. Kim will also share the importance of building relationships among staff, families, and students that will motivate, engage, empower, and create success for all. She will share strategies that ignite a passion for learning, provide support and encouragement, hold high expectations for student behavior, promote parental involvement, and ensure a safe, secure environment.

Empowering Leaders

Kim will empower school leaders with ways to support and motivate staff while simultaneously ensuring that they are creating classrooms that promote student engagement, increase academic rigor, and help develop meaningful relationships. Kim has served in school leadership positions for over eighteen years, and she will provide participants with insight and effective strategies to create an optimal learning environment for all.

How to Keep the Joy in Teaching

From philosophy to implementation, learn how to focus on what is truly important for all educators to remember. In this session, participants will be motivated, inspired, and reminded of their significant, powerful role in the lives of their students. Kim will share methods for promoting student engagement, increasing rigor, developing relationships, and creating a climate and culture that inspires learning.

Lessons for Lively Learners

Learn powerful strategies and contagious ideas that will motivate all students, and discover ways to instill a love for learning in your students while still teaching the necessary skills. Kim will share classroom techniques, including songs, kinesthetic games, and unique strategies that will engage and motivate even the most restless of learners. Kim will show participants how the required curriculum can be taught in a way that reinforces academic rigor while making learning an adventure.

About the Ron Clark Academy

The Ron Clark Academy (RCA) is a highly acclaimed, nonprofit middle school located in Southeast Atlanta. The Academy has received both national and international recognition for its success in educating students with academic rigor, passion, creativity, discipline, and respect. Our fourth–eighth grade students represent various socioeconomic and academic backgrounds.

RCA seeks to extend its reach beyond its student body by having an impact upon students everywhere. Each year, thousands of educators from around the world participate in RCA's professional development training, the RCA Experience (RCA EXP), to learn how to replicate the school's style, philosophy, and success in their own schools. RCA is a demonstration school—a place where visiting educators engage in a vibrant professional development experience by observing teachers using best practices in their classrooms before participating in hands-on workshops. In the past thirteen years, more than seventy thousand superintendents, district-level administrators, and teachers have participated in RCA EXP and the RCA Signature Series to learn better ways to engage students, promote academic rigor, and create a climate and culture that promotes success.

To learn more about RCA EXP, the RCA Signature Series, and visiting the Academy, go to www.ronclarkacademy.com.

More from

DAVE BURGESS
Consulting, Inc.

Since 2012, DBCI has been publishing books that inspire and equip educators to be their best. For more information on our titles or to purchase bulk orders for your school, district, or book study, visit **DaveBurgessconsulting.com/DBCIbooks**.

More from *Like a PIRATE*™ Series

Teach Like a PIRATE by Dave Burgess
eXPlore Like a Pirate by Michael Matera
Learn Like a Pirate by Paul Solarz
Play Like a Pirate by Quinn Rollins
Run Like a Pirate by Adam Welcome

Lead Like a PIRATE™ Series

Lead Like a PIRATE by Shelley Burgess and Beth Houf
Balance Like a Pirate by Jessica Cabeen, Jessica Johnson, and Sarah Johnson
Lead beyond Your Title by Nili Bartley
Lead with Appreciation by Amber Teamann and Melinda Miller
Lead with Culture by Jay Billy
Lead with Instructional Rounds by Vicki Wilson
Lead with Literacy by Mandy Ellis

Leadership & School Culture

Culturize by Jimmy Casas
Escaping the School Leader's Dunk Tank by Rebecca Coda and Rick Jetter
From Teacher to Leader by Starr Sackstein
The Innovator's Mindset by George Couros
It's OK to Say "They" by Christy Whittlesey
Kids Deserve It! by Todd Nesloney and Adam Welcome
Live Your Excellence by Jimmy Casas
Let Them Speak by Rebecca Coda and Rick Jetter
The Limitless School by Abe Hege and Adam Dovico
Next-Level Teaching by Jonathan Alsheimer
The Pepper Effect by Sean Gaillard
The Principled Principal by Jeffrey Zoul and Anthony McConnell
Relentless by Hamish Brewer
The Secret Solution by Todd Whitaker, Sam Miller, and Ryan Donlan
Start. Right. Now. by Todd Whitaker, Jeffrey Zoul, and Jimmy Casas
Stop. Right. Now. by Jimmy Casas and Jeffrey Zoul
Teach Your Class Off by CJ Reynolds
They Call Me "Mr. De" by Frank DeAngelis
Unmapped Potential by Julie Hasson and Missy Lennard
Word Shift by Joy Kirr
Your School Rocks by Ryan McLane and Eric Lowe

Technology & Tools

50 Things You Can Do with Google Classroom by Alice Keeler and Libbi Miller
50 Things to Go Further with Google Classroom by Alice Keeler and Libbi Miller
140 Twitter Tips for Educators by Brad Currie, Billy Krakower, and Scott Rocco
Block Breaker by Brian Aspinall
Code Breaker by Brian Aspinall
Google Apps for Littles by Christine Pinto and Alice Keeler
Master the Media by Julie Smith
Reality Bytes by Christine Lion-Bailey, Jesse Lubinsky, Micah Shippee, PhD

Shake Up Learning by Kasey Bell
Social LEADia by Jennifer Casa-Todd
Stepping up to Google Classroom by Alice Keeler and Kimberly Mattina
Teaching Math with Google Apps by Alice Keeler and Diana Herrington
Teachingland by Amanda Fox and Mary Ellen Weeks

Teaching Methods & Materials

All 4s and 5s by Andrew Sharos
Boredom Busters by Katie Powell
The Classroom Chef by John Stevens and Matt Vaudrey
The Collaborative Classroom by Trevor Muir
Copyrighteous by Diana Gill
Ditch That Homework by Matt Miller and Alice Keeler
Ditch That Textbook by Matt Miller
Don't Ditch That Tech by Matt Miller, Nate Ridgway, and Angelia Ridgway
EDrenaline Rush by John Meehan
Educated by Design by Michael Cohen, The Tech Rabbi
The EduProtocol Field Guide by Marlena Hebern and Jon Corippo
The EduProtocol Field Guide: Book 2 by Marlena Hebern and Jon Corippo
Instant Relevance by Denis Sheeran
LAUNCH by John Spencer and A.J. Juliani
Make Learning MAGICAL by Tisha Richmond
Pure Genius by Don Wettrick
The Revolution by Darren Ellwein and Derek McCoy
Shift This! by Joy Kirr
Skyrocket Your Teacher Coaching by Michael Cary Sonbert
Spark Learning by Ramsey Musallam
Sparks in the Dark by Travis Crowder and Todd Nesloney
Table Talk Math by John Stevens
The Wild Card by Hope and Wade King
The Writing on the Classroom Wall by Steve Wyborney

Inspiration, Professional Growth & Personal Development

Be REAL by Tara Martin
Be the One for Kids by Ryan Sheehy
The Coach ADVenture by Amy Illingworth
Creatively Productive by Lisa Johnson
Educational Eye Exam by Alicia Ray
The EduNinja Mindset by Jennifer Burdis
Empower Our Girls by Lynmara Colón and Adam Welcome
Finding Lifelines by Andrew Grieve and Andrew Sharos
The Four O'Clock Faculty by Rich Czyz
How Much Water Do We Have? by Pete and Kris Nunweiler
P Is for Pirate by Dave and Shelley Burgess
A Passion for Kindness by Tamara Letter
The Path to Serendipity by Allyson Apsey
Sanctuaries by Dan Tricarico
The SECRET SAUCE by Rich Czyz
Shattering the Perfect Teacher Myth by Aaron Hogan
Stories from Webb by Todd Nesloney
Talk to Me by Kim Bearden
Teach Better by Chad Ostrowski, Tiffany Ott, Rae Hughart, and Jeff Gargas
Teach Me, Teacher by Jacob Chastain
Teach, Play, Learn! by Adam Peterson
TeamMakers by Laura Robb and Evan Robb
Through the Lens of Serendipity by Allyson Apsey
The Zen Teacher by Dan Tricarico

Children's Books

Beyond Us by Aaron Polansky
Cannonball In by Tara Martin
Dolphins in Trees by Aaron Polansky
I Want to Be a Lot by Ashley Savage
The Princes of Serendip by Allyson Apsey
The Wild Card Kids by Hope and Wade King
Zom-Be a Design Thinker by Amanda Fox

CPSIA information can be obtained
at www.ICGtesting.com
Printed in the USA
FSHW020212041020
74333FS

9 781951 600181